Managing Tourism in a Changing World

Managing Tourism in a Changing World provides an overview of state-of-the-art research surrounding today's tourism management. Recognising the relevance of tourism activities as major economic drivers, this book offers a significant contribution to the advancement of managerial practice in the tourism field. It is the outcome of the collective intellectual efforts of a number of scholars, with dissimilar geographical roots and backgrounds, who cultivate original research on tourism management from a variety of perspectives (economic and managerial) and using multiple methods (theory building, experimental and inductive case-based inquiries).

While drawing on multiple theoretical perspectives and adopting different epistemological paradigms and methodologies, this book answers a wide range of research questions related to a number of relevant themes in the following fields: destination management, marketing and branding, inter-organizational dynamics and corporate social responsibility in the tourism sector.

This book was originally published as a special issue of *Anatolia*.

Rodolfo Baggio has a degree in Physics and a PhD in Tourism Management. He has worked for leading information technology firms for over 20 years and presently is a Professor at Bocconi University, Milan, where he coordinates the Information and Communication Technologies area at the Master in Economics and Tourism.

Wojciech Czakon is Professor at the Faculty of Management of the University of Economics, Katowice, where he obtained his PhD in 2002. His research focuses on interorganizational relationships including social capital, networks and coopetition strategies. He is board member of the European Academy of Management, co-chair of the EURAM Doctoral Colloquium and member of the Management and Organization Sciences at the Polish Academy of Sciences.

Marcello M. Mariani holds a PhD in Business Administration and is currently Professor of Management and Marketing at the University of Bologna where he is also the Director of the Master in Business Tourism and Destination Management, ALMA Graduate School. He is a Visiting Professor at the Stern School of Business and Tisch Center for Hospitality, Tourism, and Sports Management, New York University.

Managing Tourism in a Changing World

Issues and Cases

Edited by
**Rodolfo Baggio, Wojciech Czakon and
Marcello M. Mariani**

Routledge
Taylor & Francis Group

LONDON AND NEW YORK

First published 2014
by Routledge
2 Park Square, Milton Park, Abingdon, Oxon, OX14 4RN

Simultaneously published in the USA and Canada
by Routledge
711 Third Avenue, New York, NY 10017

Routledge is an imprint of the Taylor & Francis Group, an informa business

British Library Cataloguing in Publication Data
A catalogue record for this book is available from the British Library

ISBN13: 978-0-415-83417-9

Typeset in Times New Roman
by Taylor & Francis Books

Publisher's Note
The publisher would like to make readers aware that the chapters in this book may be referred to as articles as they are identical to the articles published in the special issue. The publisher accepts responsibility for any inconsistencies that may have arisen in the course of preparing this volume for print.

Contents

v

Citation Information

The chapters in this book were originally published in *Anatolia*, volume 23, issue 1 (April 2012). When citing this material, please use the original page numbering for each article, as follows:

Chapter 2

Accommodation industry or accommodation industries? Evidence from the analysis of production processes
Cristina Bernini and Andrea Guizzardi
Anatolia, volume 23, issue 1 (April 2012) pp. 4–16

Chapter 3

Tourism flows from the Russian Federation to the European Union
Kirill Furmanov, Olga Balaeva and Marina Predvoditeleva
Anatolia, volume 23, issue 1 (April 2012) pp. 17–31

Chapter 4

Importance–performance analysis as a diagnostic tool for urban destination managers
Tony Griffin and Deborah Edwards
Anatolia, volume 23, issue 1 (April 2012) pp. 32–48

Chapter 5

The importance of diverse stakeholders in place branding: The case of "I feel Slovenia"
Maja Konecnik Ruzzier and Nusa Petek
Anatolia, volume 23, issue 1 (April 2012) pp. 49–60

Chapter 6

Unpacking the temporal dimension of coopetition in tourism destinations: evidence from Finnish and Italian theme parks
Mika Kylanen and Marcello M. Mariani
Anatolia, volume 23, issue 1 (April 2012) pp. 61–74

Chapter 7

Ranking assessment systems for responsible tourism products and corporate social responsibility practices
Mara Manente, Valeria Minghetti and Erica Mingotto
Anatolia, volume 23, issue 1 (April 2012) pp. 75–89

Chapter 8
Knowledge transfer among clustered firms: a study of Brazil
Ariani Raquel Neckel Prux Stacke, Valmir Emil Hoffmann and Helena Araujo Costa
Anatolia, volume 23, issue 1 (April 2012) pp. 90–106

Chapter 9
Business format franchise in regional tourism development
Wojciech Czakon
Anatolia, volume 23, issue 1 (April 2012) pp. 107–117

Introduction: Managing tourism in a changing world

Rodolfo Baggio, Wojciech Czakon and Marcello M. Mariani

Tourism has enjoyed a sustained rise to recognition across management and economics literatures, business practice and development policies. As a major economic driver, in recent years tourism has attracted a growing and diverse academic attention. Beyond the growing number of books, journals, papers or theses on tourism, conferences display a variety of perspectives (both economic and managerial), developed through multiple methods ranging from theory building to experimental and inductive case-based inquiries to theory testing approaches.

In order to enrich the ongoing debate on tourism management, after considering that Europe was lacking a major international academic forum specifically dedicated to tourism management issues, the European Institute of Advanced Studies in Management (EIASM) has organized – based on an original proposal crafted by Professor Marcello M. Mariani – the *1st EIASM International Conference in Tourism Management and Tourism Related Issues* in 2011.

The first edition of the conference proved very successful with almost 100 papers submitted. After an accurate double-reviewing process, a very limited number has been accepted for presentation at the conference, in line with the idea of having a high-quality intellectual forum allowing close interaction between scholars for the advancement of tourism management, scientific cross fertilization and fruitful intellectual exchanges.

Following the successful conference, this book provides an overview of state-of-the-art research in today's tourism management. The book displays three key distinctive features. First, it recognizes tourism activities as major economic drivers involving such decision makers as research stakeholders, be them managers, policy-makers or facilitators. Second, it offers a prolific heterogeneity of theoretical perspectives, methods and results so as to grasp the variety of the field, and contributes to the advancement of managerial practice in the field. Finally, it is the outcome of a collective intellectual effort of a number of scholars, with dissimilar geographical roots and backgrounds, who cultivate original research on tourism management.

Researchers aim at contributing to the advancement of managerial practice in the field, which is a distinctive trait of recent publications. The methodological rigor of studies is very closely coupled with relevance issues so that direct implications for managers and policy-makers can be inferred. Differently from many other fields of inquiry in economics and management, tourism research gathers a number of committed stakeholders, thus facing the challenge to keep up with diverse expectations.

While drawing on multiple theoretical perspectives and adopting different epistemological paradigms and research methodologies or techniques, each and every chapter of this book attempts to answer a wide range of research questions related to numerous relevant themes in the following fields: destination management, marketing and branding, performance in the hospitality sector, corporate social responsibility and interorganizational dynamics in the tourism sector.

The first chapter by **Bernini** and **Guizzardi** focuses on the accommodation industry. Their study of hotels in Emilia Romagna region provides evidence of substantial heterogeneity in hotel production processes. Therefore it suggests taking close account of accommodation industries at plural, both for research purposes and targeted policy interventions.

In the second chapter, **Furmanov**, **Balaeva** and **Predvoditeleva** scrutinize tourism flows from the Russian Federation towards the European Union in order to address a significant research gap. Within the last two decades a dramatic change in tourism flows from the Russian Federation has taken place. Based on a quantitative methodology, the chapter models, estimates and forecasts future tourist outgoing flows.

In the third chapter, **Griffin** and **Edwards** tackle diagnostic tools for urban destination managers, developing the importance-performance analysis. This managerial tool allows the identification of current problems with tourist experience and the assignment of priorities to improve performance. The authors perform a qualitative study in Sydney and Canberra and provide both methodological insights and captivating data on Australian urban tourism destinations.

The fourth chapter by **Konecnik Ruzzier** and **Petek** sheds light on place branding from a stakeholders' perspective. The starting point here is the effectiveness of the branding process implementation. Starting from the assumption that stakeholders need to support it, they propose an inclusive overall design of the process. A close relationship between the brand and Slovenian identity is examined. The authors aim at a long-term result, which is strongly grounded in a quantitative study of key stakeholder views.

Kylanen and **Mariani** develop a temporal analysis of tourism destination coopetition in the fifth chapter. This comparative study of interorganizational relationships in Italian and Finnish empirical settings reveals long-term advantages of simultaneous competition and collaboration between theme parks. They identify understanding of common benefits generated in cooperation, such as brand image or higher number of visitors, which is seen as a precondition for successful coopetition strategy.

The sixth chapter, by **Manente**, **Minghetti** and **Mingotto**, adopts a perspective of responsible tourism products coupled with corporate social responsibility practices in order to advise on ranking assessment systems. A quantitative model is developed in order to diagnose the main attributes of assessment systems and to determine their effectiveness. Interestingly, this analytic hierarchy process (AHP) model can be applied to support small firms in espousing a more responsible approach.

Seventh, **Prux Stacke**, **Hoffmann** and **Araujo Costa** examine knowledge transfers among clustered firms in Brazil. An interorganizational perspective on knowledge assets is applied to a tourism destination in southern Brazil. While important, clustered knowledge transfers have been found to not necessarily drive competitive advantage for firms. This contributes to a broader stream of research on competitive advantage of firms in clusters.

The eighth chapter, by **Czakon**, develops the business format franchise applications in regional tourism development. Through a theoretical scrutiny, it offers a replication approach to interorganizational development strategies. Among those, franchising is seen as a governance structure that brings together managerial skills and a valid business model with entrepreneurship of small firms.

Acknowledgements

In taking this work to completion, we would like to acknowledge the efforts of several people. First, we are thankful to the authors for participating in such a stimulating project. We have asked a substantial amount of work from them and they have delivered a significant amount of their time and energy. Second, we are grateful to the European Institute of Advanced Studies in Management (EIASM) for co-organizing the conference (and particularly Mrs Graziella Michelante) and all the distinguished academics, policy-makers and executives who not only gave us their persistent support, but also personally animated the *1st EIASM International Conference in Tourism Management and Tourism Related Issues*. Among them, we wish to mention Corrado Benassi, Stefania Agostini, Patrizia Cecchi, Enzo Finocchiaro and Pietro Leoni who have directly contributed to the EIASM conference. We deeply appreciate the important support that we have received from the Dean of the Faculty of Economics (University of Bologna) Prof. Corrado Benassi, the President of the Polo di Rimini (Prof. Giorgio Cantelli Forti), the President and General Manager of UNIRIMINI (Luciano Chicchi and Lorenzo Succi) and the Director of the Rimini Center for Economic Analysis (Prof. Gianluigi Pelloni) who have provided financial support for the initiative. Finally, we are profoundly thankful to our families for the constant endorsement that they have always devoted to us and to our scientific endeavour.

Accommodation industry or accommodation industries? Evidence from the analysis of production processes

Cristina Bernini and Andrea Guizzardi

Department of Statistical Sciences, University of Bologna, Via Belle Arti, 41, Bologna 40125, Italy

Production processes heterogeneity is largely recognized in tourist accommodation industry, but few empirical evidences have been reported in the literature either on the extent of the heterogeneity or on its determinants. The aim of this study was to investigate the role of environmental features in affecting heterogeneity of accommodation production processes. Using a novel administrative data-set of hotels in Emilia Romagna (ER), we estimate stochastic frontier production functions for different hotel clusters, defined by simultaneously considering seasonality, quality (star rating), and size. Results show a relevant heterogeneity due to these environmental factors, that is different *hotel industries* exist in ER. From a policy perspective, the analysis evidences the need to develop targeted interventions to different clusters of productive structures.

1. Introduction

As observed in Roller and Sinclair-Desgagné (1996), economists have historically considered firms' heterogeneity as a temporary phenomenon. The general prediction was that firms' conduct and performance would ultimately converge, as better practices and technologies get diffused and are imitated. Conversely, evidence gathered in recent years has showed that firms' conduct and performance in a given industry could remain different for a relatively long period of time. Firms' heterogeneity in tourism is certainly a central theme. A peculiarity is that tourism industry is characterized by more than one unique productive process (Leiper, 2008). Leiper's general concepts could be also applied to the accommodation industry and hotel sector, where products and production processes appear different as well. Then, we expect heterogeneity to have an important role in studies focused on hotel productivity measurement.

The accommodation literature has recognized at least four main factors being able to modify hotel possible production technology frontiers; they are seasonality, size, quality of product, and management style, generally named as *environmental factors*. In this study, we further investigate the relevance and the interactions of these environmental factors in diversifying the productive processes of heterogeneous hotels. More precisely, in investigating whether the tourism industry is (significantly) characterized by a single accommodation industry or by several accommodation industries, we address two main research questions:

Hp1:   what are the main determinants of hotel production processes heterogeneity?
Hp2:   to what extent production processes change among hotel groups?

The aim is to detect whether there are significant differences in the estimated production functions of hotel clusters, constructed by using the previous mentioned environmental variables. Furthermore, we intend to assess the role of each environmental variable in differencing (or not) the production processes. A statistically significant evidence of the heterogeneity in the production processes, due to a wide set of environmental factors, enforces theoretical considerations on the sector heterogeneity and sustains the need of cluster-specific policy interventions.

In the analysis, we suggest using the stochastic frontier approach based on a production function to specify hotel's frontier of production possibilities. Different hotel group frontiers are estimated in order to evidence the existence of significant heterogeneity in production technologies. The elasticity estimates of labour, capital, and return to scale (RTS) allow to verify for the presence of significant differences with respect to the primary production factors.

The availability of a new source of fiscal data (FiscalSectorStudy database – FSS) well supports a wider empirical analysis of the role of environmental heterogeneity on the production technology analysis. We focus on an administrative region, Emilia-Romagna (ER), because in the current Italian institutional setting, tourism policies are governed by regions. We consider a sample of 2705 accommodation structures, representing hetero-geneous hotels in terms of environmental features (size, seasonality, standards of service, and productive factors that are labour and capital, disentangled by employment categories and type of investments).

This study has some appealing novelties. Although several studies have dealt with the topic of heterogeneity in the tourism industry, we are unaware of applications which simultaneously consider hotel category, size, seasonality, and employment categories (type of management) in a unique framework. Moreover, we broaden previous research by considering a huge cross-sectional sample of enterprises made by accommodation structures that are rarely investigated in the literature and that are micro-sized low-quality hotels. The large sample size guarantees generality and robustness to empirical results.

2. Literature review

A wide literature has considered seasonality, size, quality of product, and management style as environmental factors being able to modify the hotels' possible production technologies frontier. One of the hallmarks of tourism is the cyclical demand (Murphy, 1985). Many destinations are hardly hit by seasonal and week-end peaks, followed by low demand periods. The number of hotel open days is expected to strongly affect the possibility to amortize the capital, and thus the capacity to invest and innovate the hotel product. Furthermore, seasonality plays a central role in conditioning human resource (HR) management in different destinations. Stochastic demand patterns create challenges for tourism businesses in structuring how operations are organized and how people are managed (Baum & Szivas, 2008).

As regards size, in several economic sectors small medium enterprises (SMEs) are characterized by labour-intensive technologies, whereas large enterprises (LEs) are reveal to be more capital intensive (Yang & Chen, 2009). Moreover, SMEs typically operate under higher constrained financial condition (Cabral & Mata, 2003). Thus, the budget and production process faced by SMEs would tend to shrink compared with that faced by LEs.

Unfortunately, few evidences are available for the accommodation sector because – following the European Commission official classification rules – it is almost composed by micro or small enterprises (less than 50 employees). In UK, for example, 95% of firms in the tourism industry employ fewer than 50 employees (Lashley & Rowson, 2006), while in Italy this rate rises to 99%. Being the official size definition based on the number of employees not applicable to the hospitality industry, tourism researchers and practitioners generally identify *small* hotels by using – a more appropriate – criterion based on the number of rooms (Bastakis, Buhalis, & Butler, 2004). Adopting this criterion it becomes feasible to investigate the existence of a size-effect on production processes heterogeneity, distinguishing between *small* and other accommodation structures.

A survey of the literature relating productivity and quality of service (Hope, 2007) has evidenced that increasing service quality may lead to an increase in productivity, while increasing productivity may lead to lower the service quality. However, the relationship between service quality and productivity is a quite difficult issue to be studied empirically, given the lack of standardized and objective measures of quality in services. With respect to this point, accommodation services offer an advantage, being world widely ranked by the *stars system*. Star ranking is expected to be positively correlated with productivity. The wider supply of higher value-added services, allowed by new technologies, could be a partial explanation. Technology represents an important strategic tool in achieving competitiveness and, as shown by empirical literature, hotels access to new technologies by improving the quality of provided services and not by increasing their size (Poon, 1990).

The type of hotel management further influences the performance of the accommodation sector. La Porta (2008) shows that enterprises driven by trained managers tend to use more capital and external finance and have different types of customers, encouraging innovative practices and new technology introduction. Managers are also important in driving the process by which recruitment, education, training, and a wider HR management are planned and introduced in each firm (Baum & Szivas, 2008). Conversely, Shaw and Williams (1997) observe and list some non-economic reasons connected to a better-lifestyle expectation, implying a management style in which leisure time is preferred to income. In this case, higher costs or lower productions determine inefficiency of type X (Leibenstein, 1966). In the field of applied tourism research, some authors have handled such kinds of inefficiency (Rodriguez & Gonzales, 2007), being an interesting issue for further research.

In investigating hotel production processes and efficiency determinants, the Stochastic Frontier Analysis (SFA) has been widely used [see Barros and Santos (2006) for a complete literature survey]. A more recent issue regards the possibility that environmental characteristics affect production technology, which is the case with heterogeneous production processes. This hypothesis has been investigated in the accommodation sector, showing that environmental factors are determinants of hotel production technology. Barros, Dieke, and Santos (2010) apply the SFA random frontier model (Greene, 2004, 2005) to obtain consistent frontier estimation using a sample of 12 hotels (ranging from one-star hotel with 20 rooms to four-star hotel with 250 rooms) observed for 18 years. Their analysis evidences that hotels are heterogeneous in relation to the ratio of sales to the number of rooms and gross operational profit; this heterogeneity – if considered – changes the estimates of the stochastic frontier model. Matawie and Assaf (2008) and Assaf, Barros, and Josiassen (2010), using the metafrontier approach (O'Donnell, Rao, & Battese, 2008), find that size and type of ownership affect the production technology. The result is important even if the small available sample (78 international hotels) prevents to test the impact of environmental factors simultaneously (using more than two different hotel groups).

To our knowledge, no empirical studies have investigated neither simultaneously the full set of environmental features nor to what extent heterogeneity affects productive measures among different hotel groups.

3. Methodology

The purpose of this study is to investigate the heterogeneity in the production processes faced by different hotel groups. To this aim, we suggest using a frontier production function, estimated by a stochastic parametric approach. The choice is motivated by several considerations. First, we consider tourism firms operating in a competitive market place, where inputs can be assumed exogenous to the production function. Second, considering seasonal structure is quite common that entrepreneur's family uses a part of the hotel as home. Therefore, using a cost approach it should be necessary to explicitly consider opportunity costs that are not available from accounting measures. Finally, we are interested in investigating one output product, avoiding a multi-product environment. Thus, benefits of using the cost function approach are lessened and the production parametric approach is the best to be used with respect to our settings.

The econometric models are specified as a Cobb–Douglas production function:

$$\ln y_i = \alpha + \sum_k \beta_k \ln x_{ki} + (V_i - U_i); \quad i = 1, \ldots, N, \tag{1}$$

where $\ln y_i$ is the natural logarithm of the output of hotel i and $\ln x_{ik}$ is the logarithm of input k, where $k = L, K$ represent the inputs, which are labour and capital, respectively. The βs are parameters to be estimated. The V_is are random variables that are assumed to be independent and identically distributed, $N(0; \sigma_V^2)$. The non-negative random variables U_is, which account for technical inefficiency in production, are assumed to be independently distributed, such that U_i is the truncation (at zero) of the $N(\mu_{it}; \sigma^2)$ distribution. We choose the truncated normal form because of the hypothesis that the market is competitive, that is the greater proportion of the enterprises operate close to efficiency. It is assumed that the V_is and U_is are independent random variables.

Maximum-likelihood estimates of the model parameters (β, δ, σ^2, σ_v^2) are obtained by using R package "frontier" (Version 0.996-6, written by Coelli & Henningsen). The variance parameters are defined by $\sigma_S^2 = \sigma_V^2 + \sigma^2$ and $\gamma = \sigma^2/\sigma_S^2$ originally recommended by Battese and Corra (1977). The log-likelihood function of this model is presented in the appendix of Battese and Coelli (1993).

Hypotheses on the nature of the technical inefficiency are tested using the generalized likelihood ratio (LR) statistic, λ, given by:

$$\lambda = -2[\ln(L(H_0)) - \ln(L(H_1))], \tag{2}$$

where $L(H_0)$ and $L(H_1)$ denote the value of the likelihood function under the null and alternative hypotheses, respectively. If the given null hypothesis is true, then λ has approximately a Chi-square (or a mixed Chi-square) distribution (Coelli, 1995). The LR test can also be used to test the null hypothesis that all groups of hotels can be amalgamated into a single group. The LR statistic is defined by Equation (2), where $L(H_0)$ is the value of the log-likelihood function for the stochastic frontier estimated by pooling the data for all hotels, and $L(H_1)$ is the sum of the values of the log-likelihood functions for the group production frontiers. The degrees of freedom for the Chi-square distribution is the difference between the number of parameters estimated under H_1 and H_0. As we see below, this version of LR test is used to verify the null of homogeneous production processes between hotel groups.

3.1. The Italian fiscal sector studies

In the analysis, we take advantage of a new data source, not previously used, that is the fiscal sector studies (FSSs). FSSs are an administrative database instituted by the Italian Tax Authority in 1996 to determine, within each industry, adequate annual fiscal return for each enterprise based on accounting data, employment, structural facilities, and implemented productive processes. FSSs collect information from micro and small enterprises. The economic subjects qualified to compile questionnaires are firms, artisans, and the self-employed, whose annual turnover ranges from 25,000 to 5,160,000 euro. As a counterpart for a return declaration evaluated as adequate, these economic subjects are made free of Tax Authority income investigation.

FSS's questionnaire is composed of four main sections, namely labour force, general structural elements, activity's specific structural elements, and accounting features. A complementary information section is also included. In the labour force section, the number of worked days is collected, distinguishing with respect to contractual status (employee, self-employed, contributing family worker, all classified as regular or temporary) and category (manager, executive, clerk, workman, apprentice, home-workers).

As regards general structural elements, FSSs collect information on the structure and the spaces used in business activities. In particular, data regard geographical location (town), type of accommodation (hotel, motel, guest house, holiday home, resort hotel), classification by stars, number of rooms (categorized in bed, and private or common bathroom), and number of beds (fixed and additional), number of arrivals and overnight stays sold, opening days over the year (with and without overnights sold). As for establishment size, the effective surface is recorded (square metres), distinguishing between areas dedicated to reception and administrative services, bar service, catering service, lounge, meeting rooms and conferences, sport areas (including wellness and fitness centres), and number of parking units. Finally, daily and weekly rates for individual customers (distinguishing by type of room and service) are collected.

With respect to activity's specific structural elements, FSSs observe organizational modes (franchise chains associated with the brand). Figures in percentage of the revenue are requested for kind of customers (individuals and groups, traded or not, by broker or tour operator) and type of services (ranging from bed accommodation to full-board, from breakfast to meal, and others services connected to leisure and business tourism). The presence of a huge list of facilities and auxiliary services is also investigated.

The accounting section reports the complete detail of the profit and loss accounts. Among complementary information, there are the potential own-use of accommodation structure, and specific costs (i.e. the purchase of external cleaning services, and leasing for buildings used in accommodation activity).

3.2. Data and variables

We investigate heterogeneity in production processes by using the FFSs data referred to ER. ER is one of the most important tourism regions in Italy, offering a wide range of tourism products (seaside, mountain, artistic, and business products). In 2005, hotel production was 29 million overnight stays, corresponding to 12% of the national market. With regard to tourism supply, ER comprises 15% of national accommodation enterprises, employing 15% of workers (ISTAT, 2005). Then, ER is an interesting area to verify our hypothesis: it is one of the main tourism destinations in Italy and its accommodation supply is largely diversified.

The analysis focuses on hotels in ER in 2005, operating under the following NACE (Economic Activities in the European Union) Rev.1 codes: 55.10.A, 55.10.B, 55.23.4 and 55.23.6, being the "accommodation sector" as defined in the FSS model here considered (named TG44U). The number of establishments returning a fulfilled FSS-TG44U was 3197. This study considers 3124 hotels excluding rooms for rent for short stay accommodation, holiday homes and apartments, bed and breakfasts, residences (NACE 55.23.4), and accommodation for students and employees with hotel-like service (NACE 55.23.6). The rationale is that they are marginal in the regional supply and intrinsically heterogeneous with respect to hotels.

We further discard 303 units with an occupancy rate lower than 18.5% (the 10th percentile value), because it is highly probable that they are managed giving more importance to leisure and lifestyle of the owners than to economic results (that is they are X-inefficient). We also exclude 116 hotels not satisfying internal coherence criteria of the questionnaire. The final sample is made up of 2705 enterprises; population coverage decreases by one-tenth, but the quality of the focus on enterprises which are fully involved in the market competition increases. The sample accounts for 58% of establishments classified in NACE sector 55.10, covering 71% of the total bed supply (Table 1). The coverage is higher for establishments from two to four stars, which are the most representative of the regional structure. In accordance with the turnover requirement, FSSs coverage is poorer for larger hotels with sales exceeding 5.16 million euro. Population data with a higher disaggregation are not available from ISTAT, limiting the possibility to analyse the representativeness of our sample with respect to other features such as seasonality of business or type of management/proprietorship.

We cluster the 2705 hotels with respect to environmental variables, which we expect to lead heterogeneity in the production process. We consider three categories defined by star rating: one- and two-star, three-star, four- and five-star. A binary criterion for seasonality is used. Following the Regional Law n. 16/2004, we classified as seasonal hotels those with less than 270 opening days during the year. Because only few of the four- and five-star hotels are seasonal, we do not consider seasonality as a clustering criterion for high-star hotels.

As discussed before, the official threshold of 50 employees, commonly used for identifying small firms, does not fit in the accommodation sector; moreover, scholars have

Table 1. Population structure and sample coverage (year 2005).

	Population		FSS sample		FSS sample used in the analysis		Coverage of the sample used in the analysis	
	Source (Istat)		Source (FSS)		Source (FSS)			
	Establishments	Beds	Establishments	Beds	Establishments	Beds	Establishments (%)	Beds (%)
1star	730	19,552	321	10,408	266	8745	36	45
2star	1347	54,397	818	40,168	677	33,518	50	62
3star	2306	158,049	1757	143,307	1567	126,305	68	80
4star	304	38,524	225	29,851	193	24,716	63	64
5star	7	1208	3	402	2	349	29	29
Total	4694	271,730	3124	224,136	2705	193,633	58	71

not reached a common agreement on the criterion to define them. In order to limit the subjective choice for the threshold of small hotels, we apply two different criteria: one (*data-oriented*) reflecting a *statistical* sample optimization purpose and the second (*context-driven*) based on the local practitioners' views. Both the criteria are used in the analysis as robustness test. Following the data-oriented *statistical* criterion, we distinguish between *micro* and *small* hotels by using as thresholds the median room value of each star-ranking categorization. This strategy allows maximizing the sample size in the smaller-sized cluster, guaranteeing estimate statistical properties. The median values are 24, 38, and 59 rooms, respectively, for one- and two-, three- and four- and five-star hotels. As for the *context-driven* criterion, we split hotels between *micro* and *small* following the Club di Prodotto. Club di Prodotto, also called *Small – High Quality – Hotel*, is a corporate-local government partnership operating in ER which only incorporates three- and four- and five-star hotels with less that 40 rooms. In the absence of a segmentation criterion officially shared at regional or national level for the one- and two-star segment, we suggest using the Greece standards as described in Bastakis et al. (2004) and classify hotels in the low category (one- and two-star) as micro if they have less than 20 rooms. Therefore, combining previous indications, we define *micro* hotels as those with less than 20 rooms in one- and two-star and those with less than 40 rooms in three- and four- and five-star groups.

Considering the previous clustering criteria simultaneously (seasonality, category, and size), 10 hotel groups return.

To estimate the frontier models, we use three inputs for labour, which are the number of working days of employed managers (*Managers*), employees who are not managers (*Employees*), other types of contractual relationships – similar to the employment relationship – for the most part involving family members, or silent partners and administrators (*Families*). Capital inputs directly used for accommodation are measured by the number of beds (*Nr Beds*) and the number of added beds (*Nr Added Beds*), counting for beds that during seasonal peaks are added to those officially present in rooms. The capital inputs not directly used in guest accommodation are measured in terms of structure surface (square metres) distinguishing between reception services (*Halls*), bars, and restaurant services (*F&B*), and other services such as conference rooms, sports facilities, swimming pools, and spas (*Facilities*). A statistical summary of the variables used in this analysis is presented in Table 2, considering either the *context driven* or the *statistical* clustering criteria for hotel size. These average figures indicate that there are considerable differences between the 10 groups regarding the inputs used in the productive process, suggesting that there may exist different production processes in the accommodation sector located in ER. Less difference is detected by using the two size classifications.

4. Results

In the analysis, we use a Cobb–Douglas stochastic frontier production function to represent the production technology for hotels. Either for the whole sample of hotels (pool), assuming a homogeneous production process for all firms, or for any of the kth group, the estimated production frontier function is

$$\ln y_i = \beta_0 + \beta_1 \ln \text{Employees}_i + \beta_2 \ln \text{Families}_i + \beta_3 \ln \text{Managers}_i + \beta_4 \ln \text{NrBeds}_i$$
$$+ \beta_5 \ln \text{NrAddedBeds}_i + \beta_6 \ln F\&B_i + \beta_7 \text{Halls}_i + \beta_8 \ln \text{Facilities}_i + (v_i - u_i)$$
$$i = 1, \dots, N_j, \tag{3}$$

Table 2. Group characteristics with respect to capital and labour (mean values) and following the two different criteria for size.

Group ID	Group description	# Hotels	Employees (# days worked)	Families (# days worked)	Managers (# days worked)	# Beds	# Added beds	S_mt F&B	S_mt halls	S_mt facilities
Data-driven criterion for "small" size										
Group 1	1 and 2 stars; ≤ 24 rooms; seas.	429	226	260	11	32	3	78	39	1
Group 2	1 and 2 stars; ≤ 24 rooms; not seas.	104	410	690	42	27	2	65	34	7
Group 3	1 and 2 stars; > 24 rooms; seas.	374	473	294	26	62	4	121	57	10
Group 4	1 and 2 stars; > 24 rooms; not seas.	36	1336	755	117	63	3	59	53	11
Group 5	3 stars; ≤ 38 rooms; seas.	591	531	346	24	56	4	132	72	15
Group 6	3 stars; ≤ 38 rooms; not seas.	206	855	731	118	43	3	99	62	18
Group 7	3 stars; > 38 rooms; seas.	621	1182	388	49	109	7	223	123	52
Group 8	3 stars; > 38 rooms; not seas.	148	2532	659	205	110	7	153	132	52
Group 9	4 and 5 stars; ≤ 59 rooms	102	2248	544	167	79	4	161	122	78
Group 10	4 and 5 stars; > 59 rooms	94	4771	498	531	182	11	277	256	282
	Full sample	2705	976	413	70	72	5	144	85	34
Context-Driven criterion for "small" size										
Group 1	1 and 2 stars; ≤ 20 rooms; seas.	273	190	254	12	28	3	70	37	1
Group 2	1 and 2 stars; ≤ 20 rooms; not seas.	84	389	674	41	25	1	66	34	8
Group 3	1 and 2 stars; > 20 rooms; seas.	530	419	288	21	56	4	113	53	8
Group 4	1 and 2 stars; > 20 rooms; not seas.	56	1037	755	91	55	3	59	47	8
Group 5	3 stars; ≤ 40 rooms; seas.	671	554	345	24	59	5	136	74	16
Group 6	3 stars; ≤ 40 rooms; not seas.	223	917	730	118	46	3	98	64	18
Group 7	3 stars; > 40 rooms; seas.	542	1248	395	53	114	7	231	128	55
Group 8	3 stars; > 40 rooms; not seas.	131	2644	651	216	114	7	162	137	56
Group 9	4 and 5 stars; ≤ 40 rooms	25	1564	540	143	47	2	96	92	36
Group 10	4 and 5 stars; > 40 rooms	170	3757	522	372	141	8	236	201	197
	Full sample	2705	976	413	70	72	5	144	85	34

where ln indicates the natural logarithm, y_i the value added to hotel i. The explanatory variables are labour and capital inputs previously described. Zero observations in the dataset are handled using the approach suggested by Battese (1997). The v_is are random variables assumed to be independent and identically distributed, $N(0; \sigma_V^2)$, independent of u_is. The u_is are assumed to be independently distributed non-negative random variables, obtained by the truncation (at zero) of the $N(\mu; \sigma^2)$ distribution.

4.1. *Group frontier and pooled frontier estimates*

In order to answer the first research question, the stochastic frontier models, as defined in Equation (3), are estimated using data on hotels from the $k = 1, 2, \ldots, 10$ groups. Several checks have been made to verify model specification.

First, the null hypothesis that the technical inefficiency effects are not present, given the specifications of the stochastic frontier model, is rejected for all groups. Then, we examine whether all the groups share the same technology. A LR test of the null hypothesis, that the group stochastic frontier models are the same for all firms, is carried out after estimating the stochastic frontier by pooling the data from all 10 groups. The values of the LR statistics are highly significant (1051 and 1018, respectively, under the *data-oriented* and *context-oriented* clustering procedures), suggesting that it is not appropriate to consider the ER hotels as an industry with a single production process. Therefore, we show a significant role of seasonality, size, and star ranking in determining heterogeneity in the production processes.

If different accommodation industries exist, the next step is to investigate the role of seasonality, size, and star ranking in differentiating the hotel technology possibilities. With this aim, we test the null hypothesis of homogeneity of production function among each pair of the 10 hotel clusters. The null is strongly rejected (Table 3) for the most part of the possible pairs independently from the size-classification criteria used. A relevant exception is determined by seasonality. Three non-seasonal clusters merge together: one- and two-star small hotels, one- and two-star large hotels, and three-star small hotels, sharing the same stochastic frontier. Thus seasonality appears the main factor in determining production processes heterogeneity, while – in the case of hotels with less than four stars – the quality discriminates the production processes only for larger structures.

Previous LR test results enable to reduce the number of hotel groups from 10 to 8. For these groups we compare production processes through elasticity and RTS estimates, allowing to measure to what extent production processes change among hotel groups.

4.2. *Elasticity and return to scale estimates*

As expected, we find significant differences between parameter estimates of the hotel groups and the corresponding parameter estimates of the pooled (mis-specified) stochastic frontier (Table 4). In particular, pooling the hotels leads to a general overestimation of elasticities[1] and RTS. Labour elasticity is mainly overestimated in the highest rated hotel group; as regards capital elasticities, the major differences are for the three-star hotels. The framework does not change significantly with respect to the two hotel size classifications adopted except for Group 9. However, its small sample size (25 hotels following the *context-driven* criterion) combined with a high variability (that is common in firm production analysis) could affect parameters statistical significance. Then, we would suggest some cautions commenting estimates in this group. In general, while reporting complete results in Table 4, we prioritize the analysis of elasticity and RTS obtained by grouping hotels on the

Table 3. The LR tests: statistical criterion for size.

Group A	Group B	Chi-square	Decision with respect to Ho	Group A	Group B	Chi-square	Decision with respect to Ho
Group 2	Group 4	12.19	Not rejected	Groups 2, 4, 6	Group 10	30.89	Rejected
Group 2	Group 6	26.14	Not rejected	Group 3	Group 5	80.38	Rejected
Group 4	Group 6	19.46	Not rejected	Group 3	Group 7	90.56	Rejected
				Group 3	Group 8	149.72	Rejected
Group 1	Groups 2, 4, 6	158.57	Rejected	Group 3	Group 9	145.35	Rejected
Group 1	Group 3	42.05	Rejected	Group 3	Group 10	127.65	Rejected
Group 1	Group 5	111.84	Rejected	Group 5	Group 7	69.39	Rejected
Group 1	Group 7	181.68	Rejected	Group 5	Group 8	139.22	Rejected
Group 1	Group 8	196.17	Rejected	Group 5	Group 9	141.12	Rejected
Group 1	Group 9	128.46	Rejected	Group 5	Group 10	113.29	Rejected
Group 1	Group 10	85.94	Rejected	Group 7	Group 8	59.94	Rejected
Groups 2, 4, 6	Group 3	177.97	Rejected	Group 7	Group 9	155.48	Rejected
Groups 2, 4, 6	Group 5	158.42	Rejected	Group 7	Group 10	159.98	Rejected
Groups 2, 4, 6	Group 7	244.91	Rejected	Group 8	Group 9	67.90	Rejected
Groups 2, 4, 6	Group 8	107.10	Rejected	Group 8	Group 10	80.59	Rejected
Groups 2, 4, 6	Group 9	56.61	Rejected	Group 9	Group 10	27.75	Rejected

The LR tests: Context-driven criterion for size

Group A	Group B	Chi-square	Decision with respect to Ho	Group A	Group B	Chi-square	Decision with respect to Ho
Group 2	Group 4	20.45	Not rejected	Groups 2, 4, 6	Group 10	44.87	Rejected
Group 2	Group 6	19.06	Not rejected	Group 3	Group 5	111.17	Rejected
Group 4	Group 6	24.19	Not rejected	Group 3	Group 7	120.72	Rejected
				Group 3	Group 8	171.19	Rejected
Group 1	Groups 2, 4, 6	130.05	Rejected	Group 3	Group 9	100.59	Rejected
Group 1	Group 3	44.21	Rejected	Group 3	Group 10	176.88	Rejected
Group 1	Group 5	88.30	Rejected	Group 5	Group 7	82.70	Rejected
Group 1	Group 7	164.76	Rejected	Group 5	Group 8	155.30	Rejected
Group 1	Group 8	155.08	Rejected	Group 5	Group 9	78.86	Rejected
Group 1	Group 9	66.44	Rejected	Group 5	Group 10	151.53	Rejected
Group 1	Group 10	115.34	Rejected	Group 7	Group 8	56.36	Rejected
Groups 2, 4, 6	Group 3	227.74	Rejected	Group 7	Group 9	87.76	Rejected
Groups 2, 4, 6	Group 5	159.78	Rejected	Group 7	Group 10	161.03	Rejected
Groups 2, 4, 6	Group 7	223.73	Rejected	Group 8	Group 9	59.68	Rejected
Groups 2, 4, 6	Group 8	95.11	Rejected	Group 8	Group 10	68.35	Rejected
Groups 2, 4, 6	Group 9	34.41	Rejected	Group 9	Group 10	32.90	Rejected

Table 4. Elasticity and RTS estimates of the pool and group models, with respect to different size clustering criteria (data-driven and context-driven criteria).

Group ID	Group description	Labour elast.		Capital elast.		RTS	
		Data	Cont.	Data	Cont.	Data	Cont.
Group 1	1 and 2 stars; ≤ 24/20 rooms; seas.	0.84	0.94	0.59	0.59	1.43	1.53
Groups 2, 4, 6	1 and 2 stars; not seas.; 3 stars; ≤ 38/40 rooms; not seas.	0.55	0.53	0.49	0.51	1.04	1.04
Group 3	1 and 2 stars; > 24/20 rooms; seas.	0.62	0.61	0.52	0.58	1.15	1.19
Group 5	3 stars; ≤ 38/40 rooms; seas.	0.67	0.63	0.42	0.42	1.09	1.05
Group 7	3 stars; > 38/40 rooms; seas.	0.75	0.75	0.46	0.50	1.20	1.25
Group 8	3 stars; > 38/40 rooms; not seas.	0.67	0.67	0.42	0.49	1.09	1.16
Group 9	4 and 5 stars; ≤ 59/40 rooms	0.70	0.81	0.36	0.93	1.05	1.74
Group 10	4 and 5 stars; > 59/40 rooms	0.37	0.47	0.54	0.40	0.91	0.87
Pool	Full sample	0.80		0.62		1.42	

13

data-driven criterion. Finally, either in the pool or group frontiers, the RTSs are greater than 1, evidencing that hotels are able to increase their value added to more than the increase faced in the inputs. Also in this case, the estimated RTS from the pool frontier largely overestimates the group values, especially for non-seasonal and micro hotels.

In order to answer the second research question, a comparison of parameter estimates between groups is conducted. A deeper analysis of hotel groups' elasticity and RTS shows a large heterogeneity between hotels. As expected, ER accommodation industries are labour intensive, being the labour elasticity always higher than the capital elasticity. The only exception – considering as threshold the median rooms value – is Group 10 (the high-rated, high-sized hotel cluster), in which the estimated capital elasticity plays a major role in determining productivity. In fact, hotels in this cluster frequently host business tourists, offering many capital-intensive services.

Seasonality is a key factor in increasing both labour and capital elasticities. The rationale is that seasonal hotels are able to fully exploit their inputs during the season, affecting their total productivity positively.

Results do not allow defining a unique relationship between elasticity and hotel size and star rating. The first and the last groups are still of interest. Small seasonal low quality hotels (Group 1) evidence the highest labour elasticity and thus the highest RTS. Their own structural characteristics allow managing the peak in seasonal demand patterns by recruiting unskilled workers on the informal labour market (often on the entrepreneur's family). Informal workers are *hired* and *fired* without any indemnity as seasonal demand patterns change, leaving no trace on recorded data and artificially increasing the labour productivity of formal staff. Conversely, high quality hotels (Group 10) use capital and labour inputs less productively, RTS being less than 1. As Knowles and Curtis (1999) we have introduced the reference details in the References section explain, this may be related to the important role played by tour operators and low-price marketing strategies especially during the summer season.

The differences in production processes could be explained with a different labour and capital combination. In general, the larger the difference in environmental factors, the larger the difference in the used technology. However, only seasonality ever differentiates the production processes. For annual hotels, size and star rating do not always allow to detect significant differences in production processes.

5. Conclusion and implications

Accommodation is a heterogeneous industry, where several micro and small enterprises act. They differ not only with respect to size, but also with respect to environmental variables, making the analysis of the production processes very complex. In this framework, the purpose of this study was to investigate whether differences in hotels' size, star rating, and seasonality determine heterogeneity in the frontier of production techniques and, if this is the case, to analyse how large is the effect of heterogeneity on production processes faced by hotels.

On the basis of a wide sample of hotels located in ER, we estimate different stochastic frontier functions, clustering hotels by size, seasonality, and star rating simultaneously. The analysis finds out eight different accommodation industries, as we found eight hotel groups, operating under significantly different production techniques. The empirical results evidence several novel features of the accommodation sector. Seasonality is the environmental factor that most affects the hotel production process. The result is expected but this is – at our knowledge – the first time it has been demonstrated in the tourism-applied literature. Size and quality are also important – as evidenced in Assaf et al. (2010) – but not for non-seasonal, medium/low star-rated, small hotels, which we find sharing the same technology in ER.

The difference in production processes could be explained with different labour and capital combinations. In general, the larger the differences in environmental factors are, the larger the differences in the way inputs are combined. Seasonality is a key factor that increases both labour and capital elasticities; while the inputs mix does not change uniformly as quality and size increase. Labour return overcomes capital return almost always; only high-rated large-size hotels exhibit a capital return greater than labour. Estimating a unique – mis-specified – pooled production function leads to a general overestimation of elasticities and RTSs of the hotels in ER. Labour elasticity is mainly overestimated in the highest rated hotel group; as regards capital elasticities, the major differences are found for the three-star hotels.

Even if limited to a particular empirical context, the above results cast some doubts on various elasticity measures proposed in the literature, pooling heterogeneous firms in a unique sample. Given the relevance of such parameters in the economic analysis and policy planning, these results are fully relevant for the local policy maker. Local governments should be discouraged in supporting the regional accommodation sector as an undifferentiated industry. Conversely, this analysis evidences the need to develop targeted interventions because hotels with dissimilar category, size, and – mainly – seasonality are likely to react differently to diverse policies.

Acknowledgements

Financial support from Seneca SpA (project "Statistical Analysis of Firms' Travel Databases") is gratefully acknowledged.

Note

1. The labour elasticity is obtained by summing parameter estimates referred to: Managers, Employees and Families. The capital elasticity is calculated as the sum of parameter estimates related to: Nr Beds, Nr Added Beds, Halls, F&B and Facilities.

References

Assaf, A., Barros, C.P., & Josiassen, A. (2010). Hotel efficiency: A bootstrapped metafrontier approach. *International Journal of Hospitality Management, 29*, 468–475.

Barros, C.P., Dieke, P.U.C., & Santos, C.M. (2010). Heterogeneous technical efficiency of hotels in Luanda, Angola. *Tourism Economics, 16*(1), 137–151.

Barros, C.P., & Santos, C.A. (2006). The measurement of efficiency in Portuguese hotels with DEA. *Journal of Hospitality & Tourism Research, 30*, 378–400.

Bastakis, C., Buhalis, D., & Butler, R. (2004). The perception of small and medium sized tourism accommodation providers on the impacts of the tour operators' power in Eastern Mediterranean. *Tourism Management, 25*, 151–170.

Battese, G.E. (1997). A note on the estimation of Cobb–Douglas production functions when some explanatory variables have zero values. *Journal of Agriculture Economics, 48*, 250–252.

Battese, G.E., & Coelli, T.J. (1993). *A stochastic frontier production function incorporating a model for technical inefficiency effects.* Working Papers in Econometrics and Applied Statistics, 69. Armidale: Department of Econometrics, University of New England.

Battese, G.E., & Corra, G.S. (1977). Estimation of a production frontier model: With application to the pastoral zone of Eastern Australia. *Australian Journal of Agricultural Economics, 21*, 169–179.

Baum, T., & Szivas, E. (2008). HRD in tourism: A role for government? *Tourism Management, 29*, 783–794.

Cabral, L., & Mata, J. (2003). On the evolution of the firm size distribution: Facts and theory. *American Economic Review, 93*, 1075–1090.

Coelli, T.J. (1995). Estimators and hypothesis tests for a stochastic: A Montecarlo analysis. *Journal of Productivity Analysis, 6*, 247–268.

Greene, W. (2004). Distinguishing between heterogeneity and efficiency: Stochastic frontier analysis of the World Health Organisation's panel data on national health care systems. *Health Economics, 13*, 959–980.

Greene, W. (2005). Fixed and random effects in stochastic frontier models. *Journal of Productivity Analysis, 23*, 7–32.

Hope, C. (2007). Is there an inverse relationship between service quality and productivity or not? It's all in the definition! In P. Keller & T. Bieger (Eds.), *Productivity in tourism* (pp. 111–122). Berlin: Erich Schmidt Verlag.

ISTAT (2005). Capacità e movimento degli esercizi alberghieri. Last modified June, 2011, http://www.istat.it/imprese/turtrasp/.

Knowles, T., & Curtis, S. (1999). The market viability of European mass tourist destinations. A post-stagnation life-cycle analysis. *International Journal of Tourism Research, 1*, 87–96.

La Porta, R. (2008). *The unofficial economy and economic development.* NBER Working Paper 14520. Cambridge, MA.

Lashley, C., & Rowson, B. (2006). *The Trials and Tribulations of Hotel Ownership in Blackpool: Highlighting the skill gaps of owner managers.* CHME Research Conference. Nottingham: Nottingham Trent University.

Leibenstein, H. (1966). Allocative efficiency vs. "X-efficiency". *American Economic Review, 56*(3), 392–415.

Leiper, N. (2008). Why 'the tourism industry' is misleading as a generic expression: The case for the plural variation, tourism industries. *Tourism Management, 29*(2), 237–251.

Matawie, K.M., & Assaf, A. (2008). A metafrontier model to assess regional efficiency differences. *Journal of Modelling in Management, 3*(3), 268–276.

Murphy, P. (1985). *Tourism: A community approach.* New York: Methuen.

O'Donnell, C.J., Rao, D., & Battese, G.E. (2008). Metafrontier frameworks for the study of firm-level efficiencies and technology ratios. *Empirical Economics, 34*, 231–255.

Poon, A. (1990). Flexible specialization and small size: The case of Caribbean tourism. *World Development Volume, 18*(1), 109–123.

Roller, L.H., & Sinclair-Desgagné, B. (1996). On the heterogeneity of firms. *European Economic Review, 40*, 531–539.

Rodriguez, J.V.P., & Gonzales, E.A. (2007). Cost efficiency of the lodging industry in the tourist destination of Gran Canaria (Spain). *Tourism Management, 28*, 993–1005.

Shaw, G., & Williams, A. (1997). *The rise and fall of British coastal resorts: Cultural and economic perspectives.* London: Pinter.

Yang, C., & Chen, E. (2009). Are small firms less efficient? *Small Business Economics, 32*, 375–395.

Tourism flows from the Russian Federation to the European Union

Kirill Furmanov[a], Olga Balaeva[b] and Marina Predvoditeleva[b]

[a]Faculty of Economics, National Research University Higher School of Economics, 20 Myasnitskaya Ulitsa, Moscow 101000, Russia; [b]Faculty of Management, National Research University Higher School of Economics, 20 Myasnitskaya Ulitsa, Moscow 101000, Russia

In the last 20 years, the development of the Russian tourism industry has resulted in a dramatic change in the growth of the number of trips made by Russian citizens abroad, including tourist trips to the European Union (EU) countries; however, there is little research concerning outbound tourism from Russia. This study analyses the current trends in tourism flows from Russia to the EU countries. In order to elucidate the factors that determine the observed trends and changes in intensity of tourism flows, an econometric model of outbound flows of Russian tourists to the EU countries is estimated. Next, tourism flows in the short-term perspective are forecasted.

1. Introduction

Until the early 1990s, the tourism industry in the USSR was primarily represented by internal tourism and, to a much lesser extent, by outbound and inbound tourism. Outbound and inbound tourism were poorly developed mostly because of political reasons. The formation of a new system of market relationships in the post-Soviet Russia had an undeniably positive impact on the tourism industry and market development. Among the forces that influenced the transformation of the Russian tourism industry in the beginning of the 1990s, the most notable include the fall of the Iron Curtain, the abolition of the state monopoly on certain types of business activities, the privatization of government-owned enterprises, price liberalization, the creation of a legislative and legal framework for domestic businesses, favoured nations status to foreign businesses operating in Russia, and others.

Thus, the modernization of the Russian economy in the 1990s led to a dramatic reform in the tourism industry and the market as a whole, as evidenced by the increasing number of operating travel companies, the expanding list of available tourist destinations, the competition between Russian tourism industry players, and the increasing flows of foreign tourists into Russia. At present, Russia is one of the largest suppliers of tourists to foreign tourism markets. According to official data from the Federal State Statistics Service of Russia, the total number of trips made by Russian citizens to non-CIS countries in 2010 amounted to 25,487 thousand versus 9819 thousand trips in 2000. This included 12,231 thousand trips for tourism purposes in 2010, whereas in 2000 this number was only 4252 thousand (GKS).

Important recipients of Russian tourists are the European Union (EU) countries. On the whole, 2496 thousand Russians visited the EU countries as tourists in 2000 (GKS). This number has steadily grown, reaching 4085 thousand in 2010. The share of tourist trips to the EU countries amounted to 33% of the total number of Russian citizens' tourist trips to non-CIS countries.[1]

Thus, the European market is presently very attractive to Russian tourists. Moreover, the projected distribution of tourism flows from Russia between the EU countries actually defines the challenges that Russian and European tourism and hospitality players will face in coming years. Hence, the strategic development of the Russian and European tourism industries is greatly affected by the tourism demand of Russian citizens for different EU destinations.

Tourism demand forecasting has attracted the attention of tourism researchers and practitioners since the early 1970s (see, e.g. Andrawis, Atiya, & El-Shishiny, 2011; Armstrong, 1972; Geurts, Buchman, & Ibrahim, 1976; Jackman & Greenidge, 2010; Li, Song, & Witt, 2005; Li, Wong, Song, & Witt, 2006; Song & Li, 2008; Witt & Witt, 1995).

Unfortunately, there are virtually no studies based on Russian data, which is most likely due to the scarcity and inaccessibility of this information. A recent study (Bednova & Ratnikova, 2011) has partly filled this gap by providing an econometric model of inbound tourism in Russia.

Our paper presents the results of a quantitative analysis of outbound tourism from Russia to the EU. This paper proceeds as follows. The introduction indicates the lack of research in forecasting outbound tourism flows from Russia to the EU. Section 2 contains a literature review of the topic. Section 3 is focused on the data and methodology used in this research. In Section 4, we describe the econometric model of the demand for tourism to the EU countries and present a short-term forecast of tourism flows from Russia to the EU countries. Section 5 summarizes the conclusions, implications, limitations, and main directions of future research.

2.   Literature review

A variety of approaches have been used to forecast tourism demand. The choice of a certain forecasting technique depends on data availability, time horizons, and research objectives. These techniques can be classified into two general categories: qualitative and quantitative methods.

Detailed reviews of the different studies on tourism modelling and forecasting could be found, for example in Frechtling (2001), Song and Li (2008), and Vanhove (2011). Qualitative methods are less popular in academic literature on tourism demand forecasting. A study published by Song & Li (2008) states that "In the 121 post-2000 empirical studies... quantitative forecasting techniques were applied in all except two studies" (p. 204). However, that should not be considered as the evidence of superiority of quantitative methods over qualitative methods, because both have their own advantages and limitations that are pointed out below.

2.1.   *Qualitative forecasting methods*

Qualitative forecasting methods (also called "judgemental methods" or "subjective forecasting") rely on the judgements of experts in the specific field. These methods could be useful in several cases when quantitative analysis would have little explanatory power, which can occur in instances in which the previous trends are expected to be changed, if new factors occur that cannot be considered with mathematical methods or if insufficient statistical data are available (see, for example Frechtling, 2001; Lee, Song, & Mjelde, 2008; Vanhove, 2011).

Qualitative techniques that are used in tourism demand forecasting include traditional approaches, the Delphi method, and judgement-aided models (Frechtling, 2001; Uysal & Crompton, 1985). As Uysal and Crompton (1985) state, "Two *traditional* qualitative *approaches* to forecasting, which have been used frequently, are (1) the analysis of national or regional vacation surveys and (2) survey inquiries of the potential visitors in tourism-generating areas" (pp. 7–8). The *Delphi method* is aimed at forming a group of anonymous experts' opinions by having these experts answer questionnaires in several rounds. After each round, the experts get the aggregated report on the round and are asked to revise their answers. The Delphi method is rather popular and is also used for tourism demand forecasting. *Judgement-aided predictions* are generated during face-to-face discussions by experts whose intent is to reach a consensus on future forecasts (committee meetings, seminars, or colloquia).

Among the qualitative methods, the Delphi method seems to be the most popular. Thus, Lee and Kim (1998) used the Delphi model to predict international tourism demand for the World Cup games that were held in 2002 in Korea. Another study (Liu, 1988) uses the Delphi method to depict the results of long-term tourism forecasting in Hawaii.

There are several studies that combine quantitative and qualitative methods (for example Prideaux, Laws, & Faulkner, 2003). A recent study (Lee, Song, & Mjelde, 2008) also uses both quantitative and qualitative methods to predict the number of visitors to an international tourism Expo that is to be held in Korea in 2012.

It is a common perception that quantitative techniques (including, as a rule, time-series and causal models (Witt & Witt, 1995)) provide more accurate short-time forecasts than judgemental forecasts (see, for example Choy, 1984). Moreover, "most qualitative forecasting methods are better for medium- and long-term projections than quantitative models. They are more flexible and open to more explanatory factors" (Vanhove, 2011, p. 166).

2.2. *Quantitative forecasting methods*

Most studies that are devoted to the quantitative analysis of tourism flows can be divided into three groups. The first group includes studies that are aimed at tourism demand forecasting in a particular country or a group of countries based on time series models. The second deals with the causal econometric models that are used to explain the dynamics of tourism flows and elucidate the relationships that exist between the demand for tourism and the different factors that possibly affect it. The constructed models can also be used for forecasting purposes. The third group consists of comparative studies whose purpose is to determine the forecasting methods that outperform others in most cases. In this section, we present a short review of each of the groups of studies.

2.2.1. *Time series models*

Time series models attempt to extrapolate time series without using any information but the data on the historical behaviour of tourism flows, which often leads to results that are more accurate than those obtained using complex causal models. Extrapolating requires the assumption that the dynamics of tourism flow in the future will have the same tendencies as those depicted in recent time; however, in fact, any quantitative method implies that assumption.

Among the various techniques of univariate time series modelling, the Box–Jenkins approach based on the AutoRegressive Integrated Moving Average (ARIMA) class of models (Box & Jenkins, 1970) seems to be the most popular. One of the earliest attempts to use ARIMA models for tourism demand can be found in Geurts, Buchman, and Ibrahim (1976). More recent works include those of Lim and McAleer (2001), Balogh, Kovacs, Chaiboonsri, and Chaitip (2009), and Chaovanapoonphol, Lim, McAleer, and Wiboonpongse (2010). Exponential smoothing and different naive methods provide a useful alternative to the Box–Jenkins approach (Bhattacharya, 2011).

There is no doubt that forecasting the flow of tourism is of a great practical use and that a time series model often allows for accurate predictions. Nevertheless, forecasts themselves do not contribute much to academic knowledge. The forecast is usually exclusively based on the observed tendencies, regularities, and serial correlations that are revealed regardless of processes that underlie changes in tourism flows. This is why techniques that use univariate analysis are primarily found in comparative studies that are devoted to determining the forecasting performance of different methods.

2.2.2. Causal models of tourism demand

Measuring the direction and strength of the relationships between the demand for tourism and the various explanatory variables may provide us with information on the main determinants of tourism flows and improve our understanding of tourism market mechanisms.

The demand for tourism is measured by the number of arrivals or nights stayed, or by tourism expenditures. Among the influential factors that are usually taken into account include prices in the countries of origin and destination, exchange rates between these countries, and the consumer's income.

An early example of a causal model of tourism and its application to long-term forecasting can be found in Edwards (1988). The model used therein explains the variation of tourism expenditures in the country of origin by changes in private consumption expenditures and in the cost of travel abroad relative to domestic prices. In later works, the set of explanatory variables is usually enhanced, wherein different measures for prices and income are used; additional factors, such as dummy variables indicating special situations (for example years of political instability), are included in the models; and trend variables are used to capture unmeasured factors that lead to a stable increase or decrease in demand.

A wide range of studies that have focused on tourism demand for a particular country have been published over the course of the last 20 years. Thus, an econometric model of demand for tourism to Australia is presented in Crouch et al. (1992). Another study (Costa et al., 1994) considers the application of a demand model for the short-term forecasting of tourism flows to and from Italy. The case of Greece is studied by Dritsakis and Athanasiadis (2000), whereas the case of Russia is studied by Algieri (2006) and Bednova and Ratnikova (2011). Furthermore, another study (Lim & McAleer, 2003) concentrates on tourist arrivals from Singapore to Australia. Smeral (2004) uses the simultaneous equations approach to build up a relatively detailed world trade tourism model that explains both tourism imports and exports in monetary terms for a group of 25 countries, including Japan, the USA, and the EU.

The use of explanatory variables can also be combined with Box–Jenkins methodology, which results in the so-called ARIMAX models. Several authors find that data on consumer price indices (CPI) improve the ARIMA model of the US demand for tourism in Thailand (Chaovanapoonphol, Lim, McAleer, & Wiboonpongse, 2010).

Unfortunately, there is substantial difficulty in obtaining forecasts from causal models. Because the demand for tourism depends on explanatory variables, these variables also need to be predicted in order to calculate the forecasted value of the flow of tourism or tourism expenditures. A problem can be handled by using the vector auto regression technique, which is a multivariate analogue of the Box–Jenkins models (Song & Witt, 2006).

Less popular are the gravity models which explain the bilateral flows within a group of countries. They assume a common functional form for each pair of countries of origin and destination, which is rather restrictive. For a detailed review of gravity models, we suggest the reader to refer Paas (2000). In addition, their application to tourism analysis can be found in Armstrong (1972).

2.2.3. Comparative studies

Because there are numerous forecasting techniques that can yield different predictions, the need to compare their accuracies is obvious. The most popular way of assessing the accuracy is measuring differences between observed and predicted values of tourism flow. This leads to such measures as the mean absolute percentage error and the mean absolute scaled error. Another approach is to examine the accuracy of predicting directional changes in tourism flow dynamics or the turning point in a long-term trend (Witt & Witt, 1995). The common result of these studies is that the complex models do not outperform the simple models. ARIMA, exponential smoothing, and naive methods (assuming that the tourism flow will be constant in comparison to the corresponding previous period) prove their practical usefulness (Athanasoupulos, Hyndman, Song, & Wu, 2009; Bhattacharya, 2011; Frechtling, 2001; Song & Li, 2008; Song, Smeral, Li, & Chen, 2008; Vanhove, 2011; Witt & Witt, 1995).

3. Methodology

Our research is based on annual data provided by the Federal State Statistics Service of Russia and by the World Bank database for the period 2000–2010. It should be noted that the available statistics include data on different types of trips made by citizens for a duration of 1 day to as long as 6 months. There is a difference between business trips (including trips as service staff), trips for personal needs (e.g. educational or medical tourism), and tourist trips (holidays, participation in sporting and cultural events). In the present study, we consider trips made by Russian citizens to the EU countries for tourist purposes. We would also like to point out that our attention is restricted to the 27 countries that were EU members as of 31 December 2010. Some of the included countries joined the EU after 2000; however, in order to comply with the comparability of the data in the analysis, we use data for these countries for the entire period starting from 2000 and not only from the moment of their admission to the EU.

The number of Russian trips for tourist purposes to the EU countries has significantly grown since the previous decade; however, if we consider the share of tourist visits of Russians to the EU in the total number of trips by Russian citizens for the purpose of tourism over the world, excluding CIS countries, a steady decline can be observed: from 59% in 2000 to 33% in 2010 (see Figure 1). Amid the general rapid increase in outbound Russian citizen tourist trips, the number of European trips is growing significantly slowly, which can be explained to a certain extent by the gradual increase in the absolute number of trips to South-East Asia, North Africa, and, recently, to South America and the Caribbean. These regions are attractive to tourists because of the exoticism, novelty effect, relatively low prices, value of money, etc.

Despite an obvious interest in tours to countries that recently appeared on the Russian market, the flows of Russian tourists travelling to the EU countries are what we elected to analyse in this study.

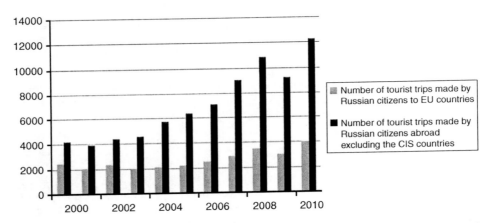

Figure 1.   Number of tourist trips made by Russian citizens to the non-CIS and the EU countries (in thousands).

The flow of Russian tourism to the EU tended to increase during the observation period; however, in some countries, there was a significant decrease. In particular, the number of tourist trips increased for Austria (sevenfold, or 616%), Greece (sevenfold, or 577%), the Netherlands (sevenfold, or 563%), and the Czech Republic (sixfold, or 496%). Some countries demonstrated a dramatic decline in tourism flows from Russia. Therein, Poland is first: the number of Russian tourists decreased by almost 22-fold (95%) from 2000 to 2010. This phenomenon derives from Russian tourists losing their interest in Polish tourism products, accompanied by a substantial complication of visa procedures. Lastly, Poland has become increasingly less attractive to the Russian shuttle trade. A decrease in the number of tourist trips made by Russians has also been observed in Estonia (11-fold, or 91%), Slovakia (5-fold, or 80%), and Lithuania (1.4-fold, or 30%), which, like in Poland, is largely due to a serious complicated visa procedure.

One should also pay attention to the significant differentiation in the number of Russian tourists visiting particular EU countries (see Figure 2). The biggest contributions, or the "big four" (more than 10% of the number of tourist trips made by Russian citizens to the EU countries), include the following: Finland, which had 709 thousand Russian tourists in 2010 (17%); Germany, which had 471 thousand (12%); Italy, which had 452 thousand (11%); and Spain, which had 411 thousand (10%). The second group (from 4% to 10%) includes Greece, the Czech Republic, Bulgaria, Cyprus, and France. Each of the remaining 18 countries, which are conditionally allocated to a third group, total no more than 4% of the number of Russians' tourist trips to the EU.

The intensity of the flow of tourism depends on many factors, some of which can only be qualitatively evaluated, whereas others have a quantitative measurement. We will further estimate the influence of traditional quantifiable factors on the Russian tourism flows to the EU.

We conduct our analysis in two steps. First, we predict the number of tourist trips to each destination country for a short-term period (by the year 2013). This forecast is obtained using univariate time series analysis methods. Next, we estimate the econometric model of demand for tourism using additional data on the prices and income of Russian consumers.

In this study, annual data for the period 2000–2010 were used. Correspondingly, we have only 11 observations per country, which is a rather small sample. The complex

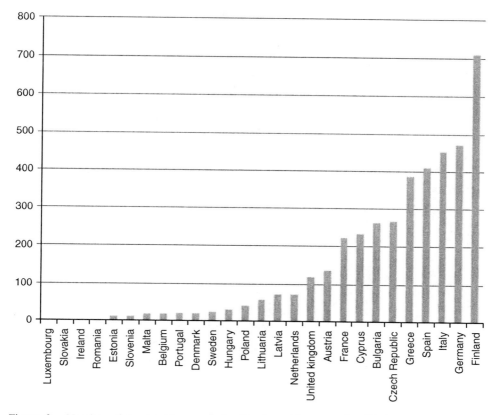

Figure 2. Number of tourist trips made by Russian citizens to the EU in 2010, by country (in thousands).

approaches that are often used for forecasting are of no use in such circumstances; therefore, the crucial factor in choosing a model is parsimony. Fortunately, that does not imply poor forecasting performance. In fact, there is some evidence that one of the best approaches to forecasting annual data on tourism is a naive method in which the forecasted values equal the tourism flow in the most recent observation (Athanasoupolos, Hyndman, Song, & Wu, 2009; Song, Smeral, Li, & Chen, 2008); however, it does not hold in case of our data because the series for most of the destination countries have obvious trend.

We make the choice in favour of the two approaches that have proven to be of great practical use in a wide range of applications. These are the Holt model and the ARIMA class of models.

The *Holt model* (Holt, 2004) is a variation on the exponential smoothing technique that allows for a trend in a series to be analysed. It has an adaptive structure (which is common for exponential smoothing models) that is useful when dealing with series that have a changing, non-stable trend. The Holt model has several modifications that are quite alike, and the modifications that were used in our study are presented below.

The observed number of tourism trips in year t ($t = 2000–2010$) is denoted F_t. Both the level estimate $\bar{F}_t$ and trend estimate T_t are calculated using the following recursive equations:

$$\bar{F}_t = \alpha(\bar{F}_{t-1} + T_{t-1}) + (1 - \alpha)F_t, \tag{1}$$

$$T_t = \beta T_{t-1} + (1 - \beta)(\bar{F}_t - \bar{F}_{t-1}). \tag{2}$$

Here, α and β are the estimated parameters and both lie between 0 and 1. These parameters represent the sensitivity of the trend and the level estimates to the data. Thus, when β is equal to 1, the trend is time-invariant; however, when β is zero, the trend in the year t is determined only by the change in the level estimates:

$$\bar{F}_t - \bar{F}_{t-1}.$$

The application of formulae (1) and (2) requires initial values of the level and trend estimates for $t = 2000$. We set the initial level estimate equal to the observed flow of tourism: $\bar{F}_{2000} = F_{2000}$. The initial trend is calculated as the average annual change in the number of tourists within the analysed period:

$$T_{2000} = \frac{F_{2010} - F_{2000}}{10}.$$

Beginning at time t and looking h years into the future, we calculate the predicted value as $\hat{F}_{t+h} = \bar{F}_t + hT_t$. The following equation has coefficients α and β that are selected to minimize the sum of squared forecast errors:

$$\sum_{t=2000}^{2009} \left(\bar{F}_t + T_t - F_{t+1} \right)^2 \underset{\alpha,\beta}{\rightarrow} \min.$$

The optimization problem is solved by the grid search method. The *Box–Jenkins' ARIMA class of models* (Box & Jenkins, 1970) seems to be the most widespread tool for short-term forecasting in econometrics. Models within ARIMA classes differ by the order of the auto-regression p, the order of the moving average q, and the order of the integration d, and they have the following formulation:

$$\Delta^d F_t = \alpha + \sum_{i=1}^{p} \beta_i(\Delta^d F_{t-i}) + \sum_{j=1}^{q} \gamma_j \varepsilon_{t-j} + \varepsilon_t. \tag{3}$$

Here, F_t is the number of tourist trips in the year t, $\alpha, \beta_1, \ldots, \beta_p, \gamma_1, \ldots, \gamma_q$ are the parameters estimated, ε_t is a random component and is assumed to be serially uncorrelated and identically distributed with a zero mean, Δ^d is a difference operator of order d.

The difference operator the first order turns the analysed series into a series of increments: $\Delta F_t = F_t - F_{t-1}$. In addition, higher-order operators can be defined by the recursive equation: $\Delta^d F_t = \Delta(\Delta^{d-1} F_t)$. Furthermore, the order of integration in a certain way depicts the nature of the trend. If $d = 0$, then it is assumed that the series has no trend.

Parameters of the ARIMA models can be estimated either by a nonlinear least squares technique, like the Holt model, or via the maximum likelihood method. The order of integration is estimated by applying various unit root tests; however, those tests have a low power in small samples. We assume that the tourism flows series are integrated in the first order, such that the mean increment in the number of tourist trips is constant.

The orders of auto-regression and of the moving average can be obtained using Akaike or Schwartz Information Criteria (Akaike, 1974; Schwarz, 1978). For the purpose of parsimony, we consider only ARIMA (1,1,0) and ARIMA (0,1,1) models with two parameters to be estimated. In this case, both criteria yield the same result of choosing the model with the lower sum of the squared forecast error.

For details on the Box–Jenkins models' estimation, we refer to Verbeek (2000).

Although both the Holt and Box–Jenkins approaches are known to be useful in forecasting, they cannot explain the reasons for changes in tourism flows. That explanation involves additional information apart from data regarding the number of tourist trips. In order to elucidate the factors that determine the intensity of tourism flow, we estimate *the regression model of demand for tourism.*

Demand for some good is usually modelled as a function of the consumer's income and the vector of prices in the economy. In practice, only the prices for the essential substitutes and complements are considered. When we speak of the demand for a tourist trip to a certain country, the tourist trip to some other country is considered to be the main substitute. Unfortunately, we do not possess data on the tourist price indices for all EU countries; thus, data on CPI are used as a proxy variable. We calculate the relative consumer price index for country i as the ratio of the CPI of that country to the CPI of the EU. We also take into account the exchange rate between the currency of the destination country and the Russian ruble.

Using annual data obtained from the Federal State Statistics Service of Russia and the World Bank from the period 1999–2010, we estimate the following separate equations for each destination country:

$$\Delta \ln F_{t+1} = \beta_0 + \beta_1 \Delta \ln \text{RI}_t + \beta_2 \Delta \ln \text{RCPI}_t + \beta_3 \Delta \ln \text{ER}_t + \varepsilon_t, \tag{4}$$

$$\ln F_{t+1} = \beta_0 + \beta_1 \ln \text{RI}_t + \beta_2 \ln \text{RCPI}_t + \beta_3 \ln \text{ER}_t + \beta_4 \text{trend}_t + \varepsilon_t, \tag{5}$$

where F_{t+1} is the number of tourist trips of Russian citizens to a country of interest in the year $t+1$, RI_t is the real money income index in Russia for year t, RCPI_t is the relative consumer price index in the destination country in year t, ER_t is the exchange rate between the currency of the destination country and the Russian ruble in year t, trend_t is a variable that stands for the trend in the data (equals 0 for $t = 1999$, equals 1 for $t = 2000$ and so on), β_0, β_1, β_2, β_3, β_4 are the estimated coefficients, and ϵ_t is the random error.

Log-linear specification is typically used for tourism demand equations (Botti, Peypoch, Randriamboarison, & Solonandrasana, 2007; Costa, Manente, Minghetti, & van der Borg, 1994; Salman, Arnesson, Sörensson, & Shukur, 2009) because it has the advantage of the convenience in interpreting the estimates. Our log-linear model coefficients β_1, β_2, and β_3 are the elasticity of the flow of tourism with respect to income, relative price, and exchange rate, respectfully (Verbeek, 2000).

Note that the dependent variable in (1) has the index $t + 1$, which means that the flow of tourism in a certain year is explained by the lagged values of the factors. Here, we follow the works of Costa and Manente (see Costa & Manente, 1994; Costa, Manente, Minghetti, & van der Borg, 1994). Therefore, explanatory variables are lagged because of the following reasons:

(1) A model is specified in such a way so as to be suitable for making forecasts for the year ahead. Although it would hardly be a real forecast because of the statistics publication lag, it could be regarded as an estimate for the number of tourist trips, which are not yet published.

(2) Taking the explanatory variables in lags helps to avoid endogeneity. The problem is that prices may be affected by the flow of tourism because of the interaction between demand and supply, which can lead to bias and inconsistency of the regression estimates; however, we suppose that the current prices are not affected by the tourism flows in the future, and so models (4) and (5) do not suffer from that problem.

The next section presents the results we obtained by estimating the tourism demand equations as well as the forecasts from the ARIMA and Holt models.

4. Results

It was supposed that the estimates obtained from (4) and (5) would reveal the relationship between the number of tourist trips and the exogenous factors. With those figures at hand, one could make forecasts assuming different scenarios of explanatory variables' dynamics. In fact, that attempt failed. Model (4) has a poor goodness-of-fit, and, for most countries, it is insignificant. Model (5) is significant with a high R^2; however, its estimated coefficients are improbable and very inaccurate because of multicollinearity.

There are numerous probable reasons for the model's inadequacy in the case of outbound tourism flows from Russia. Most of the reasons are caused by different factors, including the fact that Russia is a multinational and multicultural country with a population of 143 million people and that it occupies a territory of 17,075,400 square km with a rather significant differentiation in regional economic level. The following are some of the reasons we consider to be most important:

- CPI is likely to be a poor proxy for the tourism price index. Trip prices to the EU countries for Russian citizens significantly differ across different Russian regions because of transportation costs. For example, the distance from St. Petersburg and Moscow to the Finnish border is about 200 and 900 km, respectively, and, consequently, that makes this country one of Russia's nearest EU neighbours easy to reach from the European part of Russia, even by car. Moreover, the distance between Finland and the city of Irkutsk, which has a population of approximately 600 thousand and is situated in the East of the country, is about 6000 km, whereas the distance between Finland and Khabarovsk, which has a similar number of inhabitants, is more than 9000 km. Thus, the prices for tours to Europe and the variety of offers by travel agencies are substantially different across cities.
- The real money income index may not be an appropriate measure of a Russian consumer's income. Real money income index dynamics depict the income of an average citizen, whereas, in fact, tourists who travel to the EU are relatively rich. The income inequality in Russia is rather high: according to the official statistics, the Gini coefficient was 0.42 (GKS) in 2010; however, there are reasons to consider that estimate to have a serious biased downward trend. Thus, the average figures published by the Federal State Statistics Service of Russia may not represent the dynamics of real consumers' income.

We suppose that the model should be conducted at a more disaggregated level; however, the available statistics do not permit us to do so. Fortunately, the data do allow us to make forecasts by using univariate time-series models, which do not take into account the influence of explanatory variables. Model fit and forecasts for the five destinations that are the most popular among Russian tourists are presented in Appendix.

According to our forecasts, these countries will attract an increasing amount of Russian tourists. This holds true for most of the EU countries except for some rather unpopular destinations. Among the exceptions, Poland and Lithuania account for the largest number of tourists. The predicted number of tourist trips from Russia to the EU countries is presented in Table 1.

The tourism flows of Russian citizens to the EU countries will increase from 4085 thousand in 2010 to 4726 thousand in 2013, which is a 16% increase, as forecasted by the

Table 1.   The predicted number of tourist trips from Russia to the EU countries.

Country	2000	2010	Forecast (Holt model)		Forecast (ARIMA)	
			2013	Growth rate in % (2013–2010)	2013	Growth rate in % (2013–2010)
Austria	19	136	191	40	159	17
Belgium	5	18	21	17	21	17
Bulgaria	71	263	318	21	315	20
United Kingdom	25	120	140	17	133	11
Hungary	16	32	36	13	36	13
Germany	111	471	579	23	601	28
Greece	57	387	462	19	445	15
Denmark	6	22	28	27	27	23
Ireland	1	1	1	0	1	0
Spain	192	411	444	8	437	6
Italy	106	452	530	17	527	17
Cyprus	109	234	257	10	250	7
Latvia	24	73	80	10	77	5
Lithuania	82	58	49	−16	39	−33
Luxembourg	0	0	0	0	0	0
Malta	14	18	19	6	16	−11
Netherlands	11	73	116	59	105	44
Poland	966	43	28	−35	0	−100
Portugal	5	21	24	14	23	10
Romania	1	2	2	0	2	0
Slovakia	5	1	0	−100	0	−100
Slovenia	4	12	15	25	14	17
Finland	421	709	757	7	804	13
France	61	223	273	22	281	26
Czech Republic	45	268	326	22	325	21
Sweden	8	25	30	20	27	8
Estonia	131	12	0	−100	12	0
Total	2496	4085	4726	16	4677	14

Holt model. ARIMA predicts a slightly more moderate growth of 14%. Although the forecasts from the Holt and ARIMA models slightly differ, both techniques predict similar changes in the ranking of destination countries according to their popularity among Russian tourists. In order to not overburden our text with figures, we present the figures obtained from the Holt model, whereas forecasts from the ARIMA may be found in Table 1.

By calculating the share of the forecasted number of tourist trips to each particular EU country from the total number of tourist trips to the EU in 2013 and by classifying countries in groups according to the share of Russian tourists for a particular country in the total flow of Russian tourism to the EU in 2010 (see the Empirical setting section), we can only pinpoint several possible changes in these groups. Thus, our estimates show that there will be little changes in the relative popularity of destination countries. We expect only one shift among the leaders: by 2013, Greece can become more attractive than Spain if the observed tendencies remain. Spain will move from the leading group to the second group in 2013 because it will have less than 10% of the Russian tourism flow to the EU (from 10.1% to 9.4%), whereas Greece will almost reach this "conventional line", having 9.7% in 2013. Finland, Germany, and Italy remain the undisputed leaders.

Other expected changes in the second group seem to be minor. Thus, by 2013, Cyprus is expected to become less popular than France. This result seems to be natural because tourism flows to France were more intensive during 2003–2009, and the 2010 observation for Cyprus could be an outlier.

As for the third group, Austria, reinforcing its position as an attractive destination among Russian tourists, will move from the third to the second group as the tourism flows from Russia to Austria will change from 3.3% in 2010 to 4% in 2013. In other respects, provided there are no significant relevant changes in the economic, political, and social environment, no major changes in the "balance of power" between the tourism flows of Russians to the EU are expected.

5. Conclusion and implications

Tourism flows of Russian citizens to the EU show a steady upward trend. Moreover, there is a certain distribution of the outbound flows from Russia to the EU countries. This study presents the results of a statistical analysis of tourism flows from Russia to countries of the EU. Modelling the relationship between tourism flows from Russia to the EU countries and traditional statistically measurable factors revealed no clearly evident correlations. This lack of a correlation is possibly due to the extreme heterogeneity of Russian customers of tourist services, including the apparent income differentiation among Russian citizens, differences in preferences, differences in lifestyle, variability in the location of the place of residence relative to Europe, etc.

The available data allow us to forecast the flows of tourism from Russia to the EU countries within a short-term perspective. This study demonstrates that no major changes in the "balance of power" between EU travel destination countries are expected during the forecasted period. Finland, Germany, Italy, Greece, and Spain will remain among the leading countries that are attracting the most significant flows of Russian tourists.

Our study has several limitations. First, it considers statistical data of the Russian Federation at a national level, while Russian regions are rather heterogeneous in terms of geographical and demographical characteristics, income, customers' behaviour, etc. Second, this study is based on factors that are subject to statistical measurement only. Third, our study does not consider seasonality. Fourth, this study is focused on all of the EU countries even though there is a significant differentiation between them in terms of the role of tourism in their respective national economies and their respective orientations towards tourism. Fifth, the flows of tourism from Russia to the EU countries are investigated without taking into account the distinguishing features of the EU countries' particular regions.

Thus, the following possible directions of future research could be outlined. First, an analysis of the flows of tourism from different regions of Russia to particular EU countries should be considered. Second, expert judgements of factors that are not subject to statistical measurement and processing (for example tourists' preferences, lifestyles, and so on) are still a significant area of interest. For this purpose, qualitative research (questionnaires and/or interviews) using expert panels could be conducted. Third, a future study could be focused on an analysis of seasonal tourism flows from Russia to the EU countries or countries' regions. Fourth, the analysis, forecasting and modelling Russian tourism flows to particular EU countries and groups of countries that have been grouped according to certain criteria (for example leading countries or *vice versa* countries that demonstrate the highest rate of decline of tourism flows) could be an area of future research. Fifth, the analysis, forecasting and modelling of Russian tourism flows to particular regions of the certain EU countries appear to be a promising direction for future research.

Note

[1] Calculated according to data obtained from the Russian Federal State Statistics Service, 2010.

References

Akaike, H.A. (1974). New look at the statistical model identification. *IEEE Transactions on Automatic Control, 19*, 716–723.

Algieri, B. (2006). An econometric estimation of the demand for tourism: The case of Russia. *Tourism Economics, 12*, 5–20.

Andrawis, R.R., Atiya, A.F., & El-Shishiny, H. (2011). Combination of long term and short term forecasts, with application to tourism demand forecasting. *International Journal of Forecasting, 27*(3), 870–886.

Armstrong, C.W.G. (1972). International tourism: Coming or going? The methodological problems of forecasting. *Futures, 4*(2), 115–125.

Athanasoupulos, G., Hyndman, R.J., Song, H., & Wu, D.C. (2009). *The tourism forecasting competition* Monash Econometric and Business Statistics Working Papers, 10/08, (pp. 1–35).

Balogh, P., Kovacs, S., Chaiboonsri, C., & Chaitip, P. (2009). Forecasting with X-12-ARIMA: International tourist arrivals to India and Thailand. *Applied Studies in Agribusiness and Commerce – APSTRACT, 3*, 43–61.

Bednova, M., & Ratnikova, T. (2011). Econometric analysis of the demand for the inbound tourism in Russia. *Applied Econometrics, 21*(1), 97–113, (in Russian).

Bhattacharya, K. (2011). *Role of rules of thumb in forecasting foreign tourist arrival: A case study of India* MPRA Paper series, 28515, (pp. 1–14).

Botti, L., Peypoch, N., Randriamboarison, R., & Solonandrasana, B. (2007). An econometric model of tourism demand in France. *Tourismos: An International Multidisciplinary Journal of Tourism, 2*(1), 115–126.

Box, G., & Jenkins, G. (1970). *Time series analysis: Forecasting and control*. San Francisco, CA: Holden Day.

Chaovanapoonphol, Y., Lim, C., McAleer, M., & Wiboonpongse, A. (2010). *Time series modelling of tourism demand from the USA, Japan and Malaysia to Thailand* University of Canterbury Working Papers in Economics series, 10/05, (pp. 1–28).

Choy, D.J.L. (1984). Choy forecasting tourism revisited. *Tourism Management, 5*, 171–176.

Dritsakis, N., & Athanasiadis, S. (2000). An econometric model of tourist demand: The case of Greece. *Journal of Hospitality & Leisure Marketing, 7*(2), 39–49.

Costa, P., & Manente, M. (1994). The trip forecasting models: Theory and the case of Italy. *Tourism Review, 49*(3), 26–34.

Costa, P., Manente, M., Minghetti, V., & van der Borg, J. (1994). *Tourism demand to and from Italy: The forecasts to 1995 from the TRIP models*. Venice: Ciset.

Crouch, G., Schultz, L., & Valerio, P. (1992). Marketing international tourism to Australia: A regression analysis. *Tourism Management, 13*(2), 196–208.

Edwards, A. (1988). *International tourism forecasts to 1999*. EIU Special Report London: EIU.

Frechtling, D.C. (2001). *Forecasting tourism demand: Methods and strategies*. Oxford, UK: Butterworth-Heinemann.

Geurts, M.D., Buchman, T.A., & Ibrahim, I.B. (1976). Use of the Box-Jenkins approach to forecast tourist arrivals. *Journal of Travel Research, 14*(4), 5–8.

Holt, C.C. (2004). Forecasting seasonals and trends by exponentially weighted moving averages. *International Journal of Forecasting, 20*(1), 5–10.

Jackman, M., & Greenidge, K. (2010). Modelling and forecasting tourist flows to Barbados using structural time series models. *Tourism and Hospitality Research, 10*, 1–13.

Lee, C.K., & Kim, J.H. (1998). International tourism demand for the 2002 World Cup Korea: A combined forecasting technique. *Pacific Tourism Review, 2*(2), 1–10.

Lee, C.-K., Song, H.-J., & Mjelde, J.W. (2008). The forecasting of International Expo tourism using quantitative and qualitative techniques. *Tourism Management, 29*(6), 1084–1098.

Li, G., Song, H., & Witt, S.F. (2005). Recent developments in econometric modeling and forecasting. *Journal of Travel Research, 44*(1), 82–99.

Li, G., Wong, K.F., Song, H., & Witt, S.F. (2006). Tourism demand forecasting: A time varying parameter error correction model. *Journal of Travel Research, 45*(2), 175–185.

Lim, C., & McAleer, M. (2001). *Time series forecasts of international tourism demand for Australia* ISER Discussion Paper Series, 0533, (pp. 1–24).

Lim, C., & McAleer, M. (2003). *Modelling international travel demand from Singapore to Australia* CIRJE Discussion Paper Series, CIRJE-F-214, (pp. 1–34).

Liu, J.C. (1988). Hawaii tourism to the year 2000: A Delphi forecast. *Tourism Management, 9*(4), 279–290.

Paas, T. (2000). *Gravity approach for modeling trade flows between Estonia and the main trading partners*. Tartu: Tartu University Press.

Prideaux, B., Laws, E., & Faulkner, B. (2003). Events in Indonesia: Exploring the limits to formal tourism trends forecasting methods in complex crisis situations. *Tourism Management, 24*(4), 475–487.

Salman, A.K., Arnesson, L., Sörensson, A., & Shukur, G. (2009). *Estimating the Swedish and Norwegian international tourism demand using ISUR technique* CESIS Electronic Working Paper Series, 198, (pp. 1–55).

Schwarz, G. (1978). Estimating the dimension of a model. *The Annals of Statistics, 6*, 461–464.

Smeral, E. (2004). Long term forecasts for international tourism. *Tourism Economics, 10*(2), 145–166.

Song, H., & Li, G. (2008). Tourism demand modeling and forecasting – A review of recent research. *Tourism Management, 29*(2), 203–220.

Song, H., Smeral, E., Li, G., & Chen, J.L. (2008). *Tourism forecasting: Accuracy of alternative econometric models revisited* WIFO Working Papers, 326.

Song, H., & Witt, S.F. (2006). Forecasting international tourist flows to Macau. *Tourism Management, 27*(2), 214–224.

Uysal, M., & Crompton, J.L. (1985). An overview of approaches used to forecast tourism demand. *Journal of Travel Research, 23*(4), 7–15.

Vanhove, N. (2011). *The economics of tourism destinations*. Amsterdam: Elsevier.

Verbeek, M. (2000). *A guide to modern econometrics*. New York: Wiley.

Witt, S.F., & Witt, C.A. (1995). Forecasting tourism demand: A review of empirical research. *International Journal of Forecasting, 11*(3), 447–475.

GKS, Federal State Statistics Service (Goskomstat) of Russia., http://www.gks.ru.

WTTC. World Travel & Tourism Council, http://www.wttc.org.

Appendix: Tourism flows to the most popular destinations: actual values and forecasts

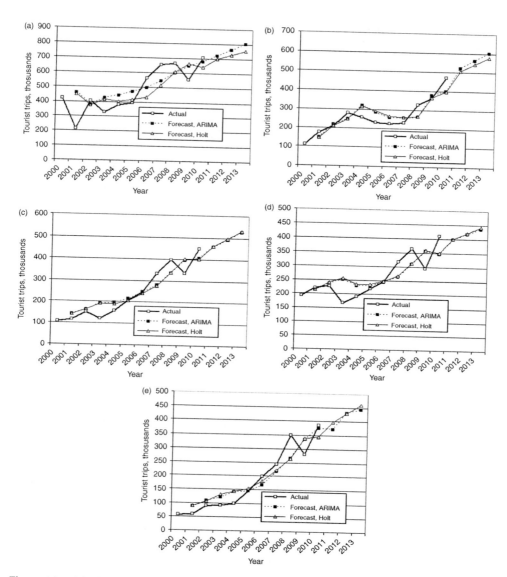

Figure A1.   (a) Finland, (b) Germany, (c) Italy, (d) Spain, and (e) Greece.

Importance–performance analysis as a diagnostic tool for urban destination managers

Tony Griffin and Deborah Edwards

Management Group, UTS Business School, University of Technology, Sydney, PO Box 222, Lindfield, NSW 2070, Australia

This paper reports on the application of importance–performance analysis to two Australian urban tourism destinations, Sydney and Canberra. The study involved asking tourists to rate the importance of 39 destination attributes and how well each destination had performed in relation to these. These importance and performance scores were then combined. From a management perspective, the most significant combination is where the destination is performing poorly in relation to attributes that tourists regard as most important. The technique represents a very useful diagnostic tool for destination managers, who can use it to identify current problems with tourist experiences and then to assign priorities to measures that are designed to improve those experiences.

1. Introduction

Managing tourist destinations is a challenging and complex process. This is especially so in cities, where the bulk of economic activities, public services, and facilities are not geared to the needs of tourists. Even the spatial layout of the city has typically evolved more in response to the needs of local residents and businesses over time rather than to tourists' needs. Understanding what tourists expect from a city experience and the features that are regarded as important to the quality of that experience can provide a partial guide to action for destination managers. Managers also need to understand how tourists perceive their current experiences, particularly features of the destination that might be currently detracting from the quality of experience.

A general method that may help to answer some of these questions is importance–performance analysis (IPA). This method, originally developed in a marketing context, has been applied to many situations, including a range of tourism products, services, and destinations. This paper reports on the application of this method to the analysis of two Australian cities as tourist destinations, Sydney and Canberra, with a view to assessing its value as a diagnostic tool for urban destination managers.

2. Literature review

IPA was initially developed by Martilla and James (1977) as a simple graphical tool to analyse customer satisfaction based on identified key attributes and perceived quality of service. The IPA approach recognizes satisfaction as a function of two components: the importance of a product or service to a customer and the performance of a business or agency in providing that service or product (Frauman & Banks, 2010). The combined customer ratings for those two components then provide an overall view of satisfaction with clear directives for management on where to focus resources and effort (Frauman & Banks, 2010). The key objective of IPA is thus diagnostic in nature, allowing managers and marketers to identify important attributes where the product or service is under- or overperforming (Abalo, Varela, & Manzano, 2007). Martilla and James (1977) also argue that customer satisfaction is influenced by expectations about the product or service attributes as well as the individual judgements of performance in relation to these same attributes. A partial approach that measures only the performance aspect leaves the marketers with a problem in translating the results of their research into marketing action.

Originally designed for marketing purposes, IPA is now used extensively in a number of areas including tourism management and destination marketing. The evaluation is usually conducted in four stages (Lai & To, 2010): (1) identifying all the key attributes of the product (or destination), (2) developing and conducting a survey to measure the perceived importance and performance of each attribute on separate Likert-based scales, (3) analysing the survey data collected by pairing the mean scores for each attribute as measured on the importance and performance scales, and (4) plotting the mean scores on a grid to assist management in decision making.

The resulting importance–performance "space" is divided into four quadrants (Bacon, 2003) where every attribute is placed according to its rating in terms of both the importance and performance scales. In Martilla and James' (1978) original analysis, the mid-points of the Likert scale were used as reference points to divide the grid into four quadrants. The analysis then depends on where the scores fall. By examining the attributes that fall within each quadrant, a manager can infer which attributes customers feel should be the highest priority for improvement and the lowest priority for action. The manager can then consider the costs of various improvements and the role that marketing can play and then develop an appropriate "action plan". This can be significant, in particular, for destination marketing and management where tourist expectations and satisfaction can significantly impact the long-term viability of the destination.

The four quadrants of the importance–performance grid consist of "concentrate here", "keep up the good work", "low priority", and "possible overkill" (see Figure 1). The first quadrant, "concentrate here", indicates attributes that are perceived to be very important to

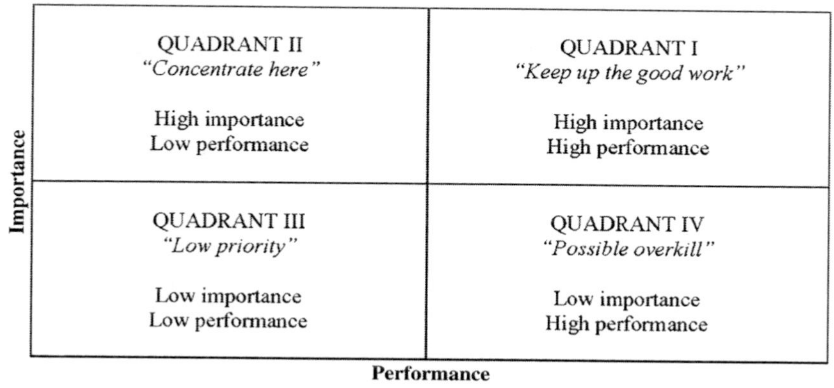

	QUADRANT II *"Concentrate here"* High importance Low performance	QUADRANT I *"Keep up the good work"* High importance High performance
	QUADRANT III *"Low priority"* Low importance Low performance	QUADRANT IV *"Possible overkill"* Low importance High performance

Importance (vertical axis label) · **Performance** (horizontal axis label)

Figure 1. IPA grid.

respondents but on which the provider does not perform well. Quadrant 2, "keep up the good work", shows attributes that are perceived to be very important, and where performance is also is rated highly. In the third quadrant, "low priority", both importance and performance of these attributes are perceived as low. Finally, "possible overkill" in quadrant 4 contains attributes that are less important but on which the provider performs well (Chu & Choi, 2000; Lai & To, 2010; Oh, 2001). In terms of management implications, IPA enables budgets and effort to be prioritized based on these outcomes. Product and service improvements should focus on attributes in the "concentrate here" quadrant, while attributes in the "possible overkill" quadrant can be the focus of cost-cutting and change management strategies (Abalo et al., 2007). In essence, the IPA provides ease of application in presenting both data and strategic suggestions in a simple graphic presentation (Martilla & James, 1977; Oh, 2001). The ease of application and the appealing method of presenting both data and strategic suggestions seem to be the main factors that have contributed to wide acceptance of the technique (Chu & Choi, 2000; Lai & To, 2010).

Researchers have applied IPA to a wide range of industrial contexts, including tourism, banking, food service, health care, education, and marketing (Almanza, Jaffe, & Lin, 1994; Cheron, McTavish, & Perrien, 1989; Cunningham & Gaeth, 1989; Ford, Joseph, & Joseph, 1999). In tourism, Evans and Chon (1989) used the IPA technique to formulate and evaluate tourism policy and Hsu, Byun, and Yang (1998) adopted the IPA technique in positioning restaurants in the leisure industry (cited in Chu & Choi, 2000). Lewis (1985, cited Chu & Choi, 2000) used IPA as a competitive analysis technique to identify tourists' perceptions of the hotel industry and Lewis and Chambers (1989) reported the effective use of IPA by the Sheraton Hotel in monitoring customer satisfaction. Similarly Joppe, Martin, and Waalen (2001) examined service providers' perceptions of customers' expectations of quality service in the hotel industry using the IPA technique. The IPA model has also been used more specifically to analyse the performance of tour guides (Zhang & Chow, 2004), escorted tours (Duke & Persia, 1996), ski resorts (Hudson & Shephard, 1998; Uysal, Howard, & Jamrozy, 1991), a marine park (Tonge & Moore, 2007), tourism policy issues (Evans & Chon, 1989), national parks (Archer & Griffin, 2004, 2005; Griffin & Archer, 2005), and destination image and attractiveness (Chon, Weaver, & Kim, 1991; Enright & Newton, 2004; Go & Zhang, 1997; Joppe, Martin, & Waalen, 2001; Litvin & Ling, 2001).

Chu and Choi (2000) argue that, in an increasingly competitive environment, a determination of a service's strengths and weaknesses is a crucial constituent of its success, and IPA can contribute to this task. According to Brieter and Milman (2006), this issue is particularly relevant to the tourism industry. The quality of service and facilities in a tourist destination are critical to its success, and crucial to establishing and maintaining a competitive edge. Service quality and customer satisfaction are principal drivers of financial performance (Deng, 2007). Matzler, Bailom, Hinterhuber, Renzl, and Pichler (2004) also maintain that customer satisfaction increases customer loyalty, reduces price sensitivity, increases cross-buying, and increases positive word of mouth, factors which can be critical to the long-term success or failure of a tourism destination. Moreover, customer satisfaction directly influences customer retention and repeat visitation (Deng & Pei, 2009).

The IPA technique, however, is not without its limitations and needs to be employed prudently. Martilla and James (1977) emphasized that the selection of attributes is critical to the effectiveness of the IPA. Excluding factors that are perceived as important to the customer will severely limit the usefulness of IPA. To avoid this, Martilla and James (1977) proposed several sources for the development of the attribute list, including previous research, qualitative research techniques (e.g. focus groups and unstructured personal interviews), and managerial judgement. These sources can be also used for screening and refining the attribute list. Likewise, Oh (2001) points to the difficulties of determining a set of attributes, particularly service attributes. Consumers may not be aware how important a particular attribute is until after they have experienced it or have experienced service failure (Oh, 2001).

There are also issues associated with the positioning of the grid lines in the IPA matrix. Martilla and James (1977) originally suggested that the positioning of the grid lines is a matter of judgement, because the value of IPA is in determining relative, rather than absolute, levels of importance and performance. The mid-point in the Likert scales could be used, but Bruyere, Rodriguez, and Vaske (2002) suggest that setting the intersection point of the matrix can also be used to provide managers with greater insight. Moving the intersection point allows for flexibility in setting standards. Positioning the grid line on the performance scale above the mid-point, for example, allows managers to set a standard of quality that significantly exceeds "neutral", and therefore reflects a higher aspiration (Hollenhorst, Olson, & Fortney, 1992; Hudson & Shephard, 1998). Adjusting the position of the grid line on the importance scale allows priorities to be more narrowly defined (Bruyere et al., 2002). Hence a destination manager with a tightly constrained budget may only want to identify issues of very high priority and could adjust the grid line so that it focuses on attributes of very high importance.

Although the IPA method has been widely applied in tourism contexts, some researchers have identified a number of conceptual and practical issues (Bacon, 2003; Deng, 2007; Oh, 2001). For example, a causal relationship may exist between importance and performance (Matzler et al., 2004; Oh, 2001; Ryan & Huyton, 2002), and hence a change in attribute performance (or satisfaction) can be associated with a change in attribute importance. As such, Oh (2001, p. 622) warns that the traditional IPA grid "could offer serious misinformation depending upon the nature and magnitude of the relationship". He therefore proposes the use of importance either as a weighting variable or the application of the causal modelling approach, whereby importance would be used as a stand-alone construct. Deng (2007) has noted that customers may only consider an attribute important if the performance of the provider in terms of that attribute is poor.

Abalo et al. (2007) suggest that another major difficulty facing IPA is the measurement of importance and performance. Generally, performance has been measured by taking the mean of the performance ratings from an appropriate group of people using a Likert scale. However, the measurement of importance is not clear-cut, and a variety of techniques have been used. Bacon (2003) and Abalo et al. (2007) identify two main techniques: a direct measure based on a similar technique used for performance, and the use of indirect measures obtained from performance ratings either by multivariate regression of an overall product or service rating or the ratings given for individual attributes. Bacon (2003) found that direct methods are more effective than indirect, but the former still have their drawbacks. Measuring importance directly is often misleading because ratings may be uniformly high (Abalo et al., 2007; Bacon, 2003). The main source of this problem is inherent in Martilla and James' (1977) procedure, in which the first steps should be to identify the most salient attributes by qualitative analysis and reviewing previous research. This has a natural tendency to result in high importance ratings on a metric (or Likert) scale for all the attributes selected for evaluation, with the result that they all crowd together at the top of the IPA grid.

Bruyere et al. (2002) have suggested that IPA has limited utility when not used in conjunction with variables to segment user groups (Vaske, Beaman, Stanley, & Grenier, 1996). IPA without this segmentation will produce results for an aggregate user group that ultimately indicates levels of satisfaction for an "average user". However, for many products (including tourist destinations) it appears that the "average user" does not really exist (Bruyere et al., 2002), and therefore average satisfaction and importance ratings are of limited practical value. Combining IPA with segmentation analysis may avoid this pitfall and the consequent misallocation of resources (Bruyere et al., 2002; Vaske et al., 1996).

In spite of these shortcomings, IPA is acknowledged as a cost-efficient and broadly applicable evaluation tool that is an attractive option for tourism managers faced with limited budgets and time constraints. IPA is inexpensive to administer, simple to interpret and, when combined with segmentation, produces results that can be incorporated into effective management strategies (Bruyere et al., 2002). Segmentation accounts for the diversity that inevitably exists between groups and potentially provides more powerful results to tourism planners and managers.

3. Methodology

A questionnaire survey was conducted in both Sydney and Canberra to determine the expectations that tourists had of their visit in relation to certain destination attributes, how important these attributes were perceived to be, and how each city performed in relation to these attributes. Sydney is Australia's most populous city and its most visited tourist destination. Canberra, by virtue of its status as national capital, receives high levels of visits from both domestic and international tourists. In accordance with recommendations by Martilla and James (1977), the attributes for inclusion in the questionnaire were selected through a combination of methods, including discussion with an industry reference group, a series of in-depth interviews with visitors to both cities, and an analysis of previous research on urban tourist destinations in which the authors had been involved (Edwards, Griffin, & Hayllar, 2007; Edwards, Small, Griffin, & Hayllar, 2008; Griffin & Hayllar, 2007, 2009; Hayllar & Griffin, 2007; Schlenker, Edwards, Hayllar, & Griffin, 2010). After piloting the questionnaire with the industry reference group and a convenience sample of tourists from outside the chosen destination cities, a total of 39 attributes were selected for inclusion in the survey. Using face validity, these attributes were grouped under five categories: city environment, city experience, range of attractions, services, and food services.

Martilla and James (1977) noted that in order to minimize compounding and order effects, the separation of the importance measures and the performance measures is recommended. By structuring the questionnaire into distinct sections, placing the importance measures in one section, and all of the performance measures in a later section, the respondent moves in a natural progression from general to more specific questions with a separation between their ratings for each attribute. In accordance with these recommendations, the questionnaire was constructed into three distinct sections that asked: the level of expectations tourists had with respect to each of these attributes, how important each attribute was to the enjoyment of their visit, and how they would rate their satisfaction with each attribute. These questions were answered in relation to the specific city they were visiting at the time, Sydney or Canberra. In each section, respondents were asked to rate each attribute on a 10-point Likert scale, with a higher number representing a higher rating. In relation to satisfaction, respondents were able to state if they did not experience an attribute.

The questionnaire also included a series of questions about the demographics of the respondent (e.g. age, gender, place of residence) and some key characteristics of their trip (e.g. trip purpose, first visit or not, trip duration, accommodation). This allowed some degree of segmentation of the responses in relation to expectations, importance, and performance, in accordance with the recommendations of Vaske et al. (1996) and Bruyere et al. (2002). The main segmentation reported on in this paper is between international and domestic tourists. Respondents were also asked to indicate their overall level of satisfaction with their experience in the city.

The survey was administered by both online and postal means. Email addresses and/or postal addresses were collected at entry points to major attractions and visitor information centres within Sydney, while an email address database, gathered during an earlier visitor research project, was used for the Canberra visitors' survey. In Sydney, fieldworkers approached tourists and asked if they would like to participate in a survey. If they agreed, their contact details were recorded and subsequently entered into a database. Within 2 and 3 weeks, they were sent a link to an online survey or posted a hard copy of the questionnaire, depending on their indicated preference at the time of recruitment. Tourists thus responded to the survey some time after their visit to Sydney or Canberra. In the case of Sydney, participant contact details were collected from early October 2008 through to early December 2008. Responses were collected from late October 2008 through to early February 2009.

In all, 3499 email invitations and 126 postal questionnaires were distributed for the Sydney sample. A total of 1018 useable responses were received (effective response rate of 28%). A total of 4609 email invitations were distributed for the Canberra sample of which 444 useable responses were received (effective response rate of 9.6%). In both cities, participants were offered the incentive of being entered in a prize draw to encourage them to respond. The difference between the sample sizes and response rates from the two cities raises obvious questions about the comparability of the findings and the reliability of the data from the smaller Canberra sample. As with any research, this study was constrained by the available funds, which led to inevitable compromises in the approach taken. Online surveys offer the advantage of relatively low administration costs, providing an appropriate database of email addresses exists. No such database existed as a sampling frame in Sydney, hence the need to recruit visitors directly for this study. However, in the case of Canberra, a database of email addresses for a large group of relatively recent visitors did exist and a decision was taken to use this as the frame for the Canberra sample. The much lower response rate from Canberra could be primarily due the longer time that elapsed between the visit and the receipt of the questionnaire, hence the details and impressions of the visit were not as fresh in the minds of the visitors. It could also be due to the fact that these visitors had not been specifically recruited for this study. Given the smaller sample size, the overall implication is that the Canberra data may not be as robust and reliable as the Sydney data. As indicated in the findings presented below, the mean scores for expectations, importance, and performance of all attributes were lower for Canberra than for Sydney, which may be a function of the greater time that had passed since the visit. However, this effect has been offset by the use of mean importance and performance scores to position the grid lines of the IPA matrix, meaning that it is relative rather than absolute ratings of the attributes that are influential.

The extensive number of questions in the three sections on expectations, importance, and performance impacted on the length of the survey and in some cases response fatigue was evident. In these cases responses were deleted. Data were entered into the Statistical Package for the Social Sciences (SPSS), version 17 for data analysis. Table 1 presents the mean scores, standard deviations, and scale α's for the variables "expectations", "importance", and "performance". It illustrates that internal reliabilities for all variables were high, with coefficient α's ranging from 0.95 to 0.97. The 39 destination attributes were grouped into five categories based on face validity: "city environment", "city

Table 1.   Mean scores, standard deviations (SD), and reliabilities (α).

Variables	No. of items	Mean[a,b]	α
Expectations	39	6.570	0.953
Importance	39	7.177	0.946
Performance	39	7.450	0.969

[a] Lower scores indicate lower levels for each variable.
[b] scale range 1–10 for each variable.

experience", "range of attractions", "services", and "food services". The high α values indicate good internal consistency among items within each category.

4.   Results

The results of the survey and the IPA are reported separately for Sydney and Canberra.

4.1.   Sydney

One thousand and eighteen useable responses were completed by visitors to Sydney. A majority of those respondents (59%) were female. The age of the respondents varied from 18 to 85 + , with the most common age of respondents falling within the 25–34 years bracket (25%). Respondents were fairly evenly spread across the 35–44, 45–54, and 55–64 brackets, each accounting for between 18% and 20% of the total sample. The majority of respondents (65%) were international visitors, with the most common countries of origin being the UK and the USA. Approximately, half of the respondents were on their first visit to Sydney and the purpose of trip for the vast majority was either a holiday (59%) or to visit friends and relatives (17%).

As indicated previously, respondents were asked to rate their perceptions of importance and performance in relation to 39 destination attributes, which were grouped under five broad categories. They were also asked to rate their level of expectations with regard to these attributes. The overall results for Sydney, grouped under the broad attribute categories, are presented in Table 2, which also compares the mean ratings for international and domestic visitors. The mean expectation scores were lower than importance and performance scores for all five categories.

A comparison of international and domestic tourists was conducted to see if there were any differences in their expectations, importance, and performance ratings across the 39 attributes. An α level of 0.05 was used for all statistical tests and r was calculated as the effect size. It was found that there was a significant difference between international and domestic tourists on their perceptions of expectations, importance, and performance in relation to a number of attributes. Very weak to moderate effect sizes were found between international and domestic tourists' expectations on 22 attributes, ratings of importance on 18 attributes, and perceptions of performance on 15 attributes. Moderate effect sizes were found for 12 attributes in the categories of city environment, city experience, and food services. The performance category of "range of attractions" had one attribute with a "large" effect size – unique history and heritage sites. That is, domestic tourists considered Sydney to perform better than did international tourists on offering a range of unique history and heritage sites.

Expectation, importance, and performance scores for domestic and international tourists were analysed in accordance with the IPA framework. The mean scores for both

Table 2. Mean scores on expectation, importance, and performance for Sydney and Canberra destination attributes for international and domestic tourists.

Attribute categories	Expectation		Importance		Performance	
	International	Domestic	International	Domestic	International	Domestic
Sydney						
City environment	6.5	6.2	6.9	6.7	7.7	7.5
City experience	6.8	5.8	7.1	6.4	7.7	7.4
Range of attractions	6.8	7.2	7.0	7.3	7.6	8.1
Services	7.5	7.6	8.3	8.4	7.9	8.0
Food services	7.3	7.4	7.9	8.3	7.9	7.8
Canberra						
City environment	5.6	5.8	6.6	6.3	7.4	7.3
City experience	5.5	5.0	6.5	5.8	7.0	6.9
Range of attractions	6.0	7.0	6.9	7.2	7.3	8.1
Services	6.2	6.2	7.7	7.2	7.0	7.3
Food services	6.8	6.0	7.8	6.8	7.4	7.3

Notes: Scale range 1–10 for each item. Higher scores indicate higher levels for each variable.

domestic and international tourists across the 39 attributes are presented in Table 3. Overall, domestic tourists had lower expectation, importance, and performance scores compared to international tourists.

Table 4 presents a comparison of the IPA grid positions for international and domestic respondents. The positioning of the grid lines was based on Deng's (2007) recommendation to use the mean of all implicitly derived degrees of importance for attributes and the mean of all performance ratings for attributes. This was primarily to avoid the problem of the scores being grouped in the upper right-hand quadrant ("keep up the good work"), given that virtually all mean scores were above the mid-point of the scale.

The five attributes with the highest performance scores among domestic respondents included museums and galleries, interesting activities, good to walk around, unique history, and easy to find attractions and services. No language barriers, good to walk around, easy to find attractions and services, good availability of food, and good availability of tourism information received the highest performance ratings by international respondents. The positive news is that Sydney can continue to keep up the good work in each of these areas.

The attributes that received the lowest ratings by domestic respondents were vibrant nightlife, relaxed local people, opportunity to meet local people, spacious urban environment, and dense built environment. Although they are low-performing attributes, when compared to their importance ratings the management of these attributes can be considered a low priority.

The most significant findings from a destination management perspective are those which are perceived to be highly important but the performance is below average. The implication is that these are the attributes where improvement is most urgent. The two attributes where Sydney needs to improve its performance for both domestic and international tourists are reasonable priced local transport and reasonable food prices. For domestic tourists, Sydney also needs to improve its performance on cleanliness, helpful local people, and providing food venues that are suitable for families.

In catering to international tourists, Sydney also needs to focus on providing good signage and opening hours that are convenient for tourists. However, it is not possible for managers to exert control over all destination attributes in equal measure such as "good weather" versus "cleanliness". Indeed the expectation score for weather was rated higher

Table 3. Expectations, importance, and performance of Sydney destination attributes.

Attribute	Domestic			International		
	Mean expectation	Mean importance	Mean performance	Mean expectation	Mean importance	Mean performance
City environment						
Cleanliness	6.50	8.14	7.36	7.14	8.19	8.18
Dense built environment	5.89	4.82	6.70	5.33	4.85	6.82
Good weather	6.74	7.16	7.89	8.07	8.04	7.66
Interesting architecture	6.51	6.96	8.06	6.61	7.15	7.85
Modern visual appeal	6.62	6.48	7.80	7.43	6.80	8.17
Old/historic visual appeal	6.81	7.23	7.99	5.59	6.82	7.38
Spacious urban environment	4.19	5.76	6.75	5.61	6.44	7.53
Variety of recreational spaces	5.92	6.84	7.54	6.18	6.84	7.92
City experience						
A relaxing place to visit	5.92	7.16	7.45	6.73	7.77	7.94
Family friendly environment	5.94	6.80	7.48	5.86	5.91	8.08
Friendly local people	5.57	7.08	7.26	7.23	8.02	7.98
Good to walk around	7.33	8.26	8.34	7.54	8.45	8.51
Helpful local people	5.89	7.32	7.41	7.15	8.12	8.03
Multicultural experience	6.01	5.84	7.20	6.80	6.88	7.40
No language barriers	6.70	6.80	8.17	8.00	7.64	8.52
Opportunity to experience local way of life	5.02	5.45	6.99	6.14	7.00	6.95
Opportunity to meet local people	4.41	5.08	6.77	6.02	6.93	7.06
Relaxed local people	4.80	6.10	6.87	6.62	7.22	7.64
Sense of excitement	6.37	6.41	7.57	6.84	6.67	7.21
Vibrant nightlife	5.26	4.80	6.92	6.03	5.28	7.02
Vibrant urban atmosphere	6.46	6.33	7.48	7.04	6.92	7.76
Range of attractions						
Interesting activities	7.77	8.00	8.42	7.48	7.83	7.95
Museums and galleries	7.71	7.60	8.48	6.94	7.06	7.85
Music and performance	6.66	6.75	7.78	6.43	6.45	7.45
Special events	6.33	6.73	7.58	6.15	6.42	7.26
Unique history	7.49	7.62	8.34	6.73	7.40	7.67
Services						
Convenient opening hours	7.83	8.27	8.25	7.35	8.14	7.62
Easy to find attractions and services	7.70	8.38	8.28	7.53	8.22	8.35
Good availability of tourism information	7.87	8.40	8.19	7.98	8.42	8.25
Good signage/directions	7.57	8.46	7.71	7.25	8.32	7.73
Local transport easy to use and understand	7.63	8.43	8.00	7.61	8.46	7.92
Reasonably priced local transport	7.17	8.41	7.64	7.17	8.24	7.55
Reliable local transport	7.58	8.50	8.08	7.53	8.45	8.18
Food services						
Family oriented	6.35	7.26	7.62	5.86	5.95	7.39
Good availability of food	8.05	8.49	8.15	7.96	8.4	8.26
Good quality	7.78	8.68	7.90	7.79	8.58	8.13
Good variety of food	7.98	8.42	8.10	7.87	8.30	8.19
Healthy and fresh	7.54	8.48	7.93	7.56	8.41	8.13
Reasonable prices	6.78	8.43	7.16	6.96	8.29	7.28

Notes: Scale range 1–10 for each item. Higher scores indicate higher levels for each variable.

Table 4. Comparison of Sydney's IPA grid positions for international and domestic tourists.

Attribute	Domestic tourists' IPA grid position	International tourists' IPA grid position
City environment		
Cleanliness	Concentrate here	Keep up the good work
Dense built environment	Low priority	Low priority
Good weather	Possible overkill	Concentrate here
Interesting architecture	Possible overkill	Possible overkill
Modern visual appeal	Possible overkill	Possible overkill
Old/historic visual appeal	Possible overkill	Low priority
Spacious urban environment	Low priority	Low priority
Variety of recreational spaces	Low priority	Possible overkill
City experience		
A relaxing place to visit	Low priority	Keep up the good work
Family friendly environment	Low priority	Possible overkill
Friendly local people	Low priority	Keep up the good work
Good to walk around	Keep up the good work	Keep up the good work
Helpful local people	Concentrate here	Keep up the good work
Multicultural experience	Low priority	Low priority
No language barriers	Possible overkill	Keep up the good work
Opportunity to experience local way of life	Low priority	Low priority
Opportunity to meet local people	Low priority	Low priority
Relaxed local people	Low priority	Low priority
Sense of excitement	Low priority	Low priority
Vibrant nightlife	Low priority	Low priority
Vibrant urban atmosphere	Low priority	Low priority
Range of attractions		
Interesting activities	Keep up the good work	Keep up the good work
Museums and galleries	Keep up the good work	Possible overkill
Music and performance	Possible overkill	Low priority
Special events	Low priority	Low priority
Unique history	Keep up the good work	Low priority
Services		
Convenient opening hours	Keep up the good work	Concentrate here
Easy to find attractions and services	Keep up the good work	Keep up the good work
Good availability of tourism information	Keep up the good work	Keep up the good work
Good signage/directions	Keep up the good work	Concentrate here
Local transport easy to use and understand	Keep up the good work	Keep up the good work
Reasonably priced local transport	Concentrate here	Concentrate here
Reliable local transport	Keep up the good work	Keep up the good work
Food services		
Family oriented	Concentrate here	Low priority
Good availability of food	Keep up the good work	Keep up the good work
Good quality	Keep up the good work	Keep up the good work
Good variety of food	Keep up the good work	Keep up the good work
Healthy and fresh	Keep up the good work	Keep up the good work
Reasonable prices	Concentrate here	Concentrate here

than the performance score, which suggests that this is more about managing tourists' expectations in relation to the type of weather they may experience during a visit to Sydney.

The degree of control that managers have over important attributes is significantly different for tourist destinations as opposed to services or products. Rarely would a destination manager have a high degree of control over any specific attribute, and often they have minimal control over most. In the case cited above, the destination manager has no control over the weather, but similarly they have little or no control over the price of food services, one of the most important attributes for the visitors to Sydney and one which was positioned in the "concentrate here" quadrant of the IPA matrix. Because of a lack of direct control over prices charged in restaurants and cafes, realistically there is little that destination managers could do to address this issue, other than to bring it to the attention of relevant industry interests in an attempt to persuade them to modify current practices. There is a case for incorporating a degree of control factor into the IPA framework when applying it to tourist destinations.

4.2. *Canberra*

Four hundred and forty-four useable responses were completed by visitors to Canberra. A majority of those respondents (61%) were female. The age range of respondents was slightly narrower than for the Sydney sample, with approximately 60% in the 35–54 age bracket. The 25–34 and 55–64 age groups were also well represented, accounting for 16% and 19% of the sample, respectively. Somewhat in contrast to the Sydney sample, only 22% of the Canberra respondents were international visitors, with half of these coming from the UK and the USA. The bulk of domestic visitors were from the nearby states of New South Wales (44%) and Victoria (25%). Seventy-five per cent of respondents were on a repeat visit, suggesting that they had very well-formed expectations. Visiting for holiday purposes was less significant than for the Sydney sample (44% compared to 59%) and a quarter of all Canberra respondents were visiting friends and relatives.

As with the Sydney sample, the Canberra respondents were asked to rate their expectations and perceptions of importance and performance in relation to the 39 destination attributes. The overall results for Canberra, grouped under the broad attribute categories, are presented in Table 2, which also compares the mean ratings for international and domestic visitors. The mean expectation scores were lower than importance and performance scores for all five categories.

A comparison between international and domestic visitors to Canberra was conducted to see if there were any differences in their expectations, importance, and performance ratings across the 39 attributes. Again it was found that there was a difference between international and domestic tourists on their expectations and perceptions of importance and performance in relation to some attributes. Very weak to moderate effect sizes were found between international and domestic tourists' expectation on 13 attributes, ratings of importance on 13 attributes, and perceptions of performance on six attributes. Moderate effect sizes were found for 16 attributes in the categories of city environment, city experience, range of attractions, and food services.

Expectation, importance, and performance scores for domestic and international tourists to Canberra were also analysed in accordance with the IPA framework. The mean scores for both domestic and international tourists across the 39 attributes are presented in Table 5. Overall, domestic tourists had lower expectation, importance, and performance scores compared with international tourists.

Table 6 presents a comparison of the IPA grid positions for international and domestic visitors to Canberra. This demonstrates that Canberra is either performing well (located in the "keep up the good work" quadrant) or overperforming (located in the "possible overkill" quadrant) in relation to the majority of attributes. Museums and galleries, no language barriers and unique heritage and history were rated in the top five attributes by both international and domestic respondents. Domestic respondents felt that Canberra had

Table 5. Expectations, importance, and performance of Canberra destination attributes.

	Domestic			International		
Attribute	Mean expectation	Mean importance	Mean performance	Mean expectation	Mean importance	Mean performance
City environment						
A variety of recreational parks	6.29	7.09	7.89	5.96	6.86	7.83
Cleanliness	7.52	8.08	8.01	7.29	8.07	8.59
Dense built environment	3.63	3.91	5.82	3.8	4.17	5.78
Good weather	5.05	6.14	7.45	6.69	7.24	8.04
Interesting architecture	5.89	6.49	7.27	5.30	6.94	7.14
Modern visual appeal	6.31	6.28	7.53	5.86	6.41	7.74
Old/historic visual appeal	5.16	6.50	7.31	4.26	6.73	6.47
Spacious urban environment	6.23	6.26	7.33	5.63	6.31	7.43
City experience						
A relaxing place to visit	6.42	7.48	7.78	6.30	7.54	7.64
Family friendly environment	6.17	6.61	7.55	5.70	5.79	7.16
Friendly local people	5.17	6.55	7.15	6.49	7.67	7.70
Good to walk around	6.32	7.55	7.59	6.39	7.76	7.19
Helpful local people	5.57	6.77	7.28	6.51	7.86	7.77
Multicultural experience	4.41	4.94	6.40	5.10	5.64	6.15
No language barriers	6.80	6.26	8.28	7.23	6.50	8.48
Opportunity to experience local way of life	4.07	4.83	6.51	5.17	6.56	7.02
Opportunity to meet local people	3.93	4.70	6.49	5.57	6.49	7.27
Relaxed local people	4.45	5.68	6.88	5.79	7.00	7.65
Sense of excitement	3.88	4.98	6.21	3.93	5.29	5.79
Vibrant nightlife	2.93	3.60	5.33	3.31	4.13	4.86
Vibrant urban atmosphere	4.22	5.20	6.10	4.36	5.66	5.73
Range of attractions						
Interesting activities	7.26	7.73	8.28	6.10	7.29	7.45
Museums and galleries	8.61	8.35	8.90	7.59	7.61	8.83
Music and performance	5.54	5.91	7.10	4.93	6.00	5.97
Special events	6.25	6.61	7.69	4.90	5.94	6.45
Unique history/heritage sites	7.12	7.45	8.45	6.21	7.39	7.91
Services						
Convenient opening hours	7.05	8.02	7.71	6.64	7.91	7.22
Easy to find attractions and services	7.38	8.23	8.07	6.60	8.04	7.69
Good availability of tourism information	7.68	8.30	8.21	7.11	8.17	7.59
Good signage/directions	7.20	8.34	7.45	6.77	8.17	7.17
Local transport easy to use and understand	4.95	5.86	6.59	5.50	7.29	6.47
Reasonably priced local transport	4.72	5.79	6.72	5.34	7.16	6.72
Reliable local transport	4.66	5.87	6.54	5.33	7.20	6.43
Food services						
Family oriented	6.27	6.70	7.61	5.70	5.87	7.28
Good availability of food	7.32	8.20	7.57	7.13	8.14	7.37
Good quality	7.43	8.36	7.66	7.07	8.24	7.56
Good variety of food	7.20	8.25	7.73	7.04	8.01	7.31
Healthy and fresh	7.06	8.20	7.71	7.14	8.14	7.56
Reasonable prices	6.73	8.09	7.19	6.54	8.23	7.11

Note: Scale range 1–10 for each item. Higher scores indicate higher levels for each variable.

Table 6.   Comparison of Canberra's IPA grid positions for international and domestic tourists.

Attribute	Domestic tourists' IPA grid position	International tourists' IPA grid position
City environment		
A variety of recreational parks	Possible overkill	Possible overkill
Cleanliness	Keep up the good work	Keep up the good work
Dense built environment	Low priority	Low priority
Good weather	Low priority	Keep up the good work
Interesting architecture	Keep up the good work	Low priority
Modern visual appeal	Possible overkill	Possible overkill
Old/historic visual appeal	Concentrate here	Low priority
Spacious urban environment	Keep up the good work	Keep up the good work
City experience		
A relaxing place to visit	Keep up the good work	Keep up the good work
Family friendly environment	Possible overkill	Low priority
Friendly local people	Low priority	Keep up the good work
Good to walk around	Keep up the good work	Concentrate here
Helpful local people	Concentrate here	Keep up the good work
Multicultural experience	Low priority	Keep up the good work
No language barriers	Possible overkill	Low priority
Opportunity to experience local way of life	Low priority	Low priority
Opportunity to meet local people	Low priority	Possible overkill
Relaxed local people	Low priority	Low priority
Sense of excitement	Low priority	Low priority
Vibrant nightlife	Low priority	Low priority
Vibrant urban atmosphere	Low priority	Possible overkill
Range of attractions		
Interesting activities	Keep up the good work	Keep up the good work
Museums and galleries	Keep up the good work	Keep up the good work
Music and performance	Low priority	Low priority
Special events	Possible overkill	Low priority
Unique history/heritage sites	Keep up the good work	Keep up the good work
Services		
Convenient opening hours	Keep up the good work	Concentrate here
Easy to find attractions and services	Keep up the good work	Keep up the good work
Good availability of tourism information	Keep up the good work	Keep up the good work
Good signage/directions	Keep up the good work	Concentrate here
Local transport easy to use and understand	Possible overkill	Possible overkill
Reasonably priced local transport	Possible overkill	Possible overkill
Reliable local transport	Possible overkill	Possible overkill
Food services		
Family oriented	Keep up the good work	Possible overkill
Good availability of food	Keep up the good work	Keep up the good work
Good quality	Keep up the good work	Keep up the good work
Good variety of food	Keep up the good work	Keep up the good work
Healthy and fresh	Keep up the good work	Keep up the good work
Reasonable prices	Concentrate here	Concentrate here

interesting activities and good availability of tourism information. International respondents rated Canberra highly in terms of its cleanliness and having good weather. In all of these important attributes, Canberra was also acknowledged as performing well.

Both domestic and international respondents gave Canberra low performance ratings on sense of excitement, vibrant urban atmosphere, dense built environment, and vibrant nightlife. Multicultural experience was rated lowly by domestic respondents while international respondents rated music and performance as low. When the performance of these attributes is combined with their importance, they emerge as low priority areas for management.

The most significant management implications arise where respondents indicate that Canberra performed relatively poorly on highly important attributes. For domestic and international respondents, Canberra can improve its performance in relation to having reasonable prices for food. Domestic tourists also felt that Canberra performed relatively poorly in relation to its "old historic visual appeal", although this is not surprising in a city that is considerably less than 100 years old. Domestic tourists indicated there was room for improvement in relation to the important attribute of having "helpful local people". In satisfying the needs of international tourists, Canberra should concentrate on providing "good signage and directions" and "convenient opening hours" and improving the city's walkability.

5. Conclusion and implications

Generally, this study has demonstrated that IPA can be a useful diagnostic tool for urban destination managers. In the cases of Sydney and Canberra, the method produced fairly clear implications for action, with contrasts between the two cities that reflected their different circumstances and some of the characteristics of their tourist markets. Both cities performed adequately on most attributes, and exceeded the visitors' expectations. Sydney tended to be rated more highly on performance than Canberra, but expectations of Canberra were typically lower on most attributes, and hence this did not lead to a significantly lower level of satisfaction with the Canberra experience. In fact, the IPA grid for Sydney indicated that there were eight attributes where highly important attributes recorded relatively low levels of performance ("concentrate here") compared to six in Canberra, suggesting that the price of high expectations is that managers have to work hard to ensure that their destination lives up to them.

One difficulty of applying the IPA method to urban destinations, however, is the sheer complexity of such places and the limited degree of control that managers may exert over some attributes. An IPA may diagnose certain problems, but it is still a challenge to formulate appropriate responses to such diagnoses. Some attributes incorporated into this study, such as the weather, are simply impossible to control. In this study, international tourists in Sydney rated the weather as very important to their quality of experience but indicated that they had been disappointed with it. In such instances, the control needs to be exerted over expectations rather than performance to avoid creating disappointment by building up a destination's image beyond its capacity to deliver. With other attributes taking corrective action is possible, but extremely problematic. For instance, the attribute "helpful local people" fell into the "concentrate here" quadrant for domestic tourists in Sydney. Finding effective ways to encourage or enable Sydney residents to be more helpful is challenging to say the least. In this case, there is the additional problem that international tourists rated the helpfulness of locals highly, suggesting that Sydney residents may have different attitudes towards the different groups of tourists. In some cases, the differences between the two groups of tourists suggest specific actions if the destination marketers wish to attract more of a certain type of tourist. For instance, in Canberra, the IPA results for international tourists suggested that action was needed to improve the city's walkability, its services needed to operate with more convenient opening hours, and directional signage needed to be improved. None of these attributes emerged as problematic for the domestic market. In other instances, however, the messages are quite clear, for example, both international and domestic tourists saw problems with the pricing of Sydney's public transport. The implied action is obvious for authorities willing to take it.

Overall, the study has also revealed that there are some attributes which are likely to be regarded as highly important in most urban destinations. Of all the five categories of attribute, services were rated as most important in both cities and for both sets of tourists. Food services also rated highly in terms of importance in Sydney, but less so in Canberra, where expectations about this set of attributes tended to be somewhat lower. These attributes might be regarded as enablers rather than direct elements of a tourist experience – good signage, information services, and transport are not enjoyable in themselves, but enable the tourist to save time and money. Urban destination managers hence need to recognize that these are of fundamental importance to ensure that tourists get maximum value out of their city experience. This conclusion, however, needs to be qualified somewhat, as this study has considered only two cities in one country. To validate the importance of the services set of attributes, more research needs to be conducted across a greater range of cities, in both Australia and other parts of the world.

The high importance ratings for services also reflect the nature of tourism in cities, where visitors typically find themselves in a complex, unfamiliar environment. Regardless of the type of visitor they are, or the kind of experiences they are seeking, the vast majority of visitors share the characteristic of having a fairly short time to spend in a strange place. The only exceptions to this would be fairly frequent repeat visitors. Hence effective information, signage, and transport represent fundamental needs that most visitors share. The other sets of attributes, such as city environment, city experience, and range of attractions, are more likely to vary in importance between different groups of visitors, which will affect their average importance rating. The attribute set of food services sits somewhere in between, representing a basic need for some groups of visitors but one which may be easily satisfied given the ready availability of such services in most cities. For other visitors, however, food is a highly important qualitative part of the tourism experience, and a city's cafes and restaurants may effectively represent a significant component of its attraction base. Overall, the more experientially based attribute sets are more likely to vary depending on the tastes, preferences, and circumstances of different groups of visitors. For instance, the attribute of a vibrant nightlife may be extremely important to young single adults but totally inconsequential to families travelling with young children, yet the wide range of ratings likely to be expressed in this case will inevitably lower the overall importance rating. In this situation, the destination manager is likely to be responding to the wrong signal if relying wholly and solely on the mean importance scores alone.

Applying IPA to a tourist destination is thus an inherently more complex process than applying it to a tourism product or service. To be used effectively as a diagnostic tool for destination managers, it certainly needs to be complemented by segmentation and by an analysis of the IPA grid outcomes for various groups of visitors. Indeed there is a case for adding a third dimension to the analysis – a rating of the relative importance to the destination of various market segments. Unlike the other dimensions, this would be a management-determined rating. Factors which could influence this rating may include the proportion of current visitor nights or expenditure attributable to a defined segment, the growth prospects of the segment, and/or its contribution to reducing the degree of seasonality of visitation to the destination. Consequently management actions could be inferred where an attribute falls into the "low priority" quadrant (low importance + low performance) based on the aggregate analysis, but it is highly important to a segment which represents a rapidly growing and potentially very lucrative market for the destination. The application of IPA to complex destinations with diverse market segments seeking different experiences must thus be tempered by the exercise of considerable judgement on the part of managers if it is to be truly effective as a diagnostic tool.

References

Abalo, J., Varela, J., & Manzano, V. (2007). Importance values for importance-performance analysis: A formula for spreading out values from preference rankings. *Journal of Business Research, 60*(2), 115–121.

Almanza, B.A., Jaffe, W., & Lin, L. (1994). Use of the service attribute matrix to measure consumer satisfaction. *Journal of Hospitality and Tourism Research, 17*(2), 63–75.

Archer, D., & Griffin, T. (2004). *Visitor survey results: Barrington Tops National Park.* Gold Coast: Sustainable Tourism CRC.

Archer, D., & Griffin, T. (2005). *A study of visitor use and satisfaction in Mungo National Park.* Gold Coast: Sustainable Tourism CRC.

Bacon, D.R. (2003). A comparison of approaches to importance-performance analysis. *International Journal of Market Research, 45*, 55–77.

Brieter, D., & Milman, A. (2006). Attendees' needs and service priorities in a large convention centre: Application of the importance-performance theory. *Tourism Management, 27*(6), 1364–1370.

Bruyere, B.L., Rodriguez, D.A., & Vaske, J.J. (2002). Enhancing importance-performance analysis through segmentation. *Journal of Travel and Tourism Marketing, 12*(1), 89–95.

Cheron, E.J., McTavish, R., & Perrien, J. (1989). Segmentation of bank commercial markets. *International Journal of Bank Marketing, 6*(1), 25–30.

Chon, K., Weaver, P.A., & Kim, C.Y. (1991). Marketing your community: Image analysis in Norfolk. *The Cornell HRA Quarterly, 31*(4), 31–36.

Chu, R.K.S., & Choi, T. (2000). An importance-performance analysis of hotel selection factors in the Hong Kong hotel industry: A comparison of business and leisure travellers. *Tourism Management, 21*(4), 363–377.

Cunningham, M.A., & Gaeth, G.J. (1989). Using importance-performance analysis to assess patients' decisions to seek care in a dental school clinic. *Journal of Dental Education, 53*(10), 584–586.

Deng, W. (2007). Using a revised importance-performance analysis approach: The case of Taiwanese hot springs tourism. *Tourism Management, 28*(5), 1274–1284.

Deng, W.J., & Pei, W. (2009). Fuzzy neural based importance-performance analysis for determining critical service attributes. *Expert Systems with Applications, 36*(2), 3774–3784.

Duke, C.R., & Persia, M.A. (1996). Performance-importance analysis of escorted tour evaluations. In D. Fessenmaier (Ed.), *Recent advances in tourism marketing research* (pp. 207–223). New York: The Haworth Press.

Edwards, D., Griffin, T., & Hayllar, B. (2007). *Development of an Australian urban tourism research agenda.* Gold Coast: Sustainable Tourism CRC.

Edwards, D., Small, K., Griffin, T., & Hayllar, B. (2008). Sites of experience: The functions of urban tourism precincts. In S. Richardson, L. Fredline, A. Patiar, & M. Ternel (Eds.), *CAUTHE, Proceedings of the 18th Annual CAUTHE Conference*, CD-ROM, Griffith University, Gold Coast, 11–14 February.

Enright, M.J., & Newton, J. (2004). Tourism destination competitiveness: A quantitative approach. *Tourism Management, 25*(6), 777–788.

Evans, M.R., & Chon, K.S. (1989). Formulating and evaluating tourism policy using importance performance analysis. *Hospitality, Education and Research Journal, 13*(2), 203–213.

Ford, J.B., Joseph, M., & Joseph, B. (1999). Importance-performance analysis as a strategic tool for service marketers: The case of service quality perceptions of business students in New Zealand and the USA. *Journal of Services Marketing, 13*(2), 171–186.

Frauman, E., & Banks, S. (2010). Gateway community resident perceptions of tourism development: Incorporating importance-performance analysis into limits of acceptable change framework. *Tourism Management, 32*(1), 128–140.

Go, F.M., & Zhang, W. (1997). Applying importance-performance analysis to Beijing as an international meeting destination. *Journal of Travel Research, 35*(3), 42–49.

Griffin, T., & Archer, D. (2005). *Visitor study 1999–2000: Northern NSW national parks.* Gold Coast: Sustainable Tourism CRC.

Griffin, T., & Hayllar, B. (2007). Historic waterfronts as tourism precincts: An experiential perspective. *Tourism and Hospitality Research, 7*(1), 3–16.

Griffin, T., & Hayllar, B. (2009). Urban tourism precincts and the experience of place. *Journal of Hospitality Marketing and Management, 18*(2/3), 127–153.

Hayllar, B., & Griffin, T. (2007). A tale of two precincts. In J. Tribe & D. Airey (Eds.), *Developments in tourism research* (pp. 155–169). Oxford: Elsevier.

Hollenhorst, S., Olson, D., & Fortney, R. (1992). Use of importance-performance analysis to evaluate state park cabins: The case of the West Virginia state park system. *Journal of Park and Recreation Administration, 10*(1), 1–11.

Hudson, S., & Shephard, G.W.H. (1998). Measuring service quality at tourist destinations: An application of importance-performance analysis to an alpine ski resort. *Journal of Travel and Tourism Marketing, 7*(3), 61–77.

Hsu, C.H.C., Byun, S., & Yang, I. (1998). Attitudes of Korean college students towards quick-service, family-style, and fine dining restaurants. *Journal of Restaurant and Foodservice Marketing, 2*(4), 65–85.

Joppe, M., Martin, D.W., & Waalen, J. (2001). Toronto's image as a destination: A comparative importance-satisfaction analysis by origin of visitor. *Journal of Travel Research, 39*(3), 252–260.

Lai, L.S.L., & To, W.M. (2010). Importance-performance analysis for public management decision making: An empirical study of China's Macao Special Administrative Region. *Management Decision, 48*(2), 277–295.

Lewis, R.C., & Chambers, R.E. (1989). *Marketing leadership in hospitality*. New York: Van Nostrand Reinhold.

Litvin, S.W., & Ling, S.N.S. (2001). The destination attribute management model: An empirical application to Bintan, Indonesia. *Tourism Management, 22*(5), 481–492.

Martilla, J.A., & James, J.C. (1977). Importance-performance analysis. *Journal of Marketing, 41*(1), 77–79.

Matzler, K., Bailom, F., Hinterhuber, H.H., Renzl, B., & Pichlet, J. (2004). The asymmetric relationship between attribute-level performance and overall customer satisfaction: A reconsideration of the importance-performance analysis. *Industrial Marketing Management, 33*, 271–277.

Oh, H. (2001). Revisiting importance-performance analysis. *Tourism Management, 22*(6), 617–627.

Ryan, C., & Huyton, J. (2002). Tourists and aboriginal people. *Annals of Tourism Research, 29*(3), 631–647.

Schlenker, K., Edwards, D., Hayllar, B., & Griffin, T. (2010). *City spaces, functional places: Functions of urban tourism precincts*, CAUTHE: Proceedings of the 20th Annual CAUTHE Conference. CD-ROM, University of Tasmania, Hobart, 8–11 February.

Tonge, J., & Moore, S.A. (2007). Importance-satisfaction analysis for marine-park hinterlands: A Western Australian case study. *Tourism Management, 28*(3), 768–776.

Uysal, M., Howard, G., & Jamrozy, U. (1991). An application of importance-performance analysis to a ski resort: A case study in North Carolina. *Visions in Leisure and Business, 10*, 16–25.

Vaske, J.J., Beaman, J., Stanley, R., & Grenier, M. (1996). Importance-performance and segmentation: Where do we go from here? *Journal of Travel and Tourism Marketing, 5*(3), 225–240.

Zhang, H.Q., & Chow, I. (2004). Application of importance-performance model in tour guides performance: Evidence from mainland Chinese outbound visitors in Hong Kong. *Tourism Management, 25*(1), 81–91.

The importance of diverse stakeholders in place branding: The case of "I feel Slovenia"

Maja Konecnik Ruzzier and Nusa Petek

Marketing Department, Faculty of Economics, University of Ljubljana, Kardeljeva ploscad 17, 1000 Ljubljana, Slovenia

One of the biggest challenges in place branding lies in the ability to include stakeholders in brand building process. This is presented in the case of Slovenia, where country brand building was approached from an identity perspective. A three-step approach was employed in order to target three different groups of internal stakeholders: opinion leaders, representatives from selected key areas, and general public. Results from a quantitative study targeting 707 representatives from selected key areas are presented in the main part of the paper. Due to a strong agreement regarding brand identity elements, we assume that Slovenians share a common opinion about what the brand identity elements are. On this basis, the foundations and elements of Slovenian brand identity were built.

1. Introduction

Countries, cities, and regions have started to realize that it is very important to develop a strong brand with unique identity in order to succeed in the global marketplace. Continents, countries, cities, regions, and even smaller geographic units are usually referred as tourism destinations (Bieger, 2000; Buhalis, 2000). Destination brands are connected mainly with tourism, but nevertheless, some authors point out that destination brands include other fields as well, such as economy, culture, foreign affairs, and so on (Dinnie, 2004; Hanna & Rowley, 2008; Morgan, Pritchard, & Piggott, 2003). Since there is no generally acknowledged definition of destination brand, we use the term "destination brand" in the context of tourism, and the term "country brand" in relation to all other fields. Developing and implementing a destination brand represents a big challenge for its owners (Konecnik & Go, 2008), but developing a country brand is an even bigger challenge due to diverse stakeholder groups that represent the relevant country.

In the following paper, we present the process of developing the country brand I feel Slovenia, which is the first systematic branding process in Slovenia since its independence in 1991. The lack of an incisive story and consensus about the unique identity characteristics of Slovenia was the reason for carrying out the large-scale project in 2007, which contributed to form a basis for the Slovenia brand (Konecnik Ruzzier, 2011; Konecnik Ruzzier, Lapajne, Drapal, & de Chernatony, 2009). The final result of the brand formation process is the brand I feel Slovenia, which represents opinions of diverse stakeholders about the unique country characteristics that are similar to all fields in the county. In the paper the main idea and process of country brand building are presented. In the focal part of the paper we focus on the results of the quantitative research, which included 707 representatives from key country areas.

2. County brand – complex entity of diverse stakeholder groups

Interest in studying and analyzing country and destination brands has grown in recent years in scientific marketing literature (Cai, 2002; Konecnik, 2004; Konecnik & Gartner, 2007; Morgan & Pritchard, 2002; Pike, 2009). Core concepts of destination brands were developed from branding principles of product brands. Although a few authors were against transferring the concept of branding to the tourism destination field (O'Shaughnessy & O'Shaughnessy, 2000), the opinion of advocates of destination brands prevailed (Cai, 2002; Dinnie, 2008; Konecnik & Gartner, 2007; Pike, 2009). Nevertheless, even advocates of destination branding warn care is required when transferring product brand concepts to destination brands (de Chernatony & Dall'Olmo Riley, 1999; Konecnik Ruzzier & de Chernatony, in press). This is especially important in the case of developing destination brands, since they are formed, developed, and managed in a manner different from other brand types (Hankinson, 2007; Kavaratzis, 2005; Konecnik & Go, 2008; Pike, 2005).

Prevailing opinion in the scientific literature emphasizes that destination brand management has a lot in common with corporate brand management (Hankinson, 2007; Kavaratzis, 2005). Regardless of all the parallel characteristics of corporate and destination brands, the latter are even more complex due to the huge amount of influential stakeholders who construct tourism destinations (Buhalis, 2000; Konecnik & Go, 2008; Morgan, Pritchard, & Piggott 2002, 2003; Ryan, 2002). Nevertheless, in the process of destination brand formation, environmental specifics such as social relationships, history, and geography of the destination need to be taken into account.

How to include all influential stakeholders in the process of destination brand development and furthermore in the process of brand implementation is among the biggest challenges in destination branding. Buhalis (2000) states that additional care is needed with destination brands, since they are formed by six main stakeholder groups: tourists, the host population, the public sector and government, tourism enterprises and SMTE (small and medium-sized tourism enterprises) groups, tour operators, and other groups (environmental, cultural, etc.). All stated stakeholder groups have their own interests, benefits, and responsibilities regarding destinations. Managing destination strategies by regarding the wishes of diverse stakeholder groups and minimizing negative impacts and costs is very challenging. The challenge is even bigger due to the fact that the interests and benefits of diverse stakeholders are opposite in many cases. Therefore, Buhalis (2000) points out that dynamic relationship among stakeholder groups is needed (see Figure 1). Only cooperation among all stakeholders enables long-term success and the sustainable development of the tourism destination.

The analogy presented by Buhalis (2000) can be transferred also to the field of country branding, in which country brands are considered to be even more complex than destination brands. In the process of country brand formation, several stakeholder groups from diverse areas (such as tourism, economy, culture, and so on) need to be taken into account. Among diverse areas we need to consider various internal stakeholders, from brand owners, usually set by the local government, to local inhabitants who actively live and experience the country brand (Konecnik Ruzzier, 2011). Moreover, external

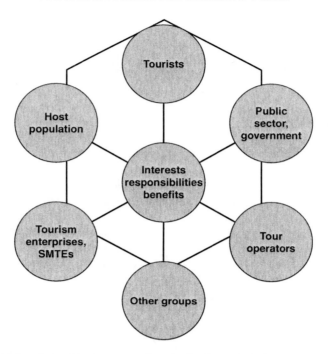

Figure 1.   Dynamic relationship among tourism destination stakeholders. *Source*: Adapted from Buhalis (2000, p. 99).

stakeholders present a very important stakeholder group, since their country brand perceptions are essential for its success (Konecnik & Gartner, 2007).

The latest scientific articles stress that strong country brands are those where the internal stakeholder groups have knowledge about the brand's identity and its main competitive advantages (de Chernatony, 1999; Konecnik Ruzzier & de Chernatony, in press; Morgan & Pritchard, 2002). Therefore, the process of country brand formation should be managed through identity view, which stresses the important role of internal stakeholder groups. It is vitally important to involve representatives from diverse internal stakeholder groups already in the brand development process and also later in the brand implementation and maintenance process (Konecnik & Go, 2008; Konecnik Ruzzier, 2011; Konecnik Ruzzier & Ruzzier, 2009). Therefore, internal stakeholder groups are of key importance for country brand co-creation and its long-term success.

3.   Methodology

3.1.   Methodology of the "I feel Slovenia" brand formation

In contrast to previous marketing activities of the brand Slovenia, which emphasized mainly visual elements of Slovenia for tourism purposes, the new brand, I feel Slovenia, represents the first systematic attempt of country brand formation (Konecnik Ruzzier, 2011), which follows recent approaches of country brand development and management. The I feel Slovenia brand formation was based on identity approach, since key stakeholder groups including representatives from tourism, economy, politics, and the civil service, science, culture and arts, sports, and the civil sphere were invited to participate in the brand formation process (Konecnik Ruzzier, 2011). The used approach can be seen as a holistic approach of Slovenia brand identity formation. The main aim was to gain suggestions and opinions of diverse stakeholder groups about Slovenia's identity and to define those identity characteristics with the highest agreement among stakeholder groups (Konecnik Ruzzier et al., 2009).

The process of Slovenia brand development consisted of four phases. In the first phase, relevant country brand identity models were reviewed and the most suitable model was chosen. Slovenia's brand identity was based on de Chernatony's (1999, 2010) brand identity model, which was additionally adapted and upgraded. Proposed brand identity elements, such as vision, values, personality, and distinguishing preferences, were enriched by two additional elements: mission and benefits. Furthermore, functional and emotional values and experiential promises were also incorporated into the model on all levels (Konecnik Ruzzier & de Chernatony, in press).

In the second phase, a review of relevant guidelines based on secondary data was conducted. Overview of previous marketing efforts of the Slovenia brand and a review of selected country brands known as good and bad country branding practices were made.

The third phase consisted of the collection of the primary data, in which representatives of all key stakeholder groups were taken into account. Considering the data collection, a three-step approach to target three different groups of respondents was followed. A Delphi study with 30 opinion leaders from all the key areas was conducted in the first phase. It was important that opinion leaders had knowledge about branding of Slovenia; therefore, the majority (21 among 30) were in positions directly related to branding of Slovenia and the rest in positions indirectly related to branding of Slovenia (Konecnik Ruzzier & de Chernatony, in press). Seventy-three point three percent of opinion leaders were male and 39.6% were female. Most opinion leaders had doctoral degree (53.3%), followed by master degree (30.0%) and university education (10.0%). Least opinion leaders had secondary or higher education (6.7%). Opinion leaders were employed in six key country areas of employment: commerce (23.3%), tourism (16.7%), science (16.7%), state and civic matters (16.7%), culture and art (16.7%), and sport (10.0%).

The Delphi study was made in two iterations and the results were used to form a questionnaire with the aim of gathering opinions from key stakeholder groups (Konecnik Ruzzier, 2009). Also, local inhabitants were asked to fill the questionnaire on the country brand website.

In the fourth phase, the Slovenia brand identity model, based on the findings of all the previous phases, was developed (Ministry of the Economy, 2007a). Opinions from quantitative research common to all key stakeholder groups present the foundation for brand identity elements. In the next step, the I feel Slovenia story, based on brand identity model, was developed. All discrepancies in opinions from diverse stakeholder groups were embodied in stories written for each key country area. Brand stories that were written are: story of Slovenians, story of Slovenia as a state, story of Slovenia as a tourist destination, and stories in the areas of economy, arts and culture, science, and sports (Ministry of the Economy, 2007a). Story of each area emphasises special characteristics of each area, but nevertheless the main identity elements and main brand story of Slovenia remain the same (Konecnik Ruzzier & de Chernatony, in press).

3.2. Methodology of quantitative research among representatives of key stakeholder groups

Representatives from all key stakeholder groups took part in quantitative research, which corresponds to the second step in the previously presented three-step approach. The aim of the quantitative research was to canvas opinions about elements of identity of the Slovenia brand from representatives of all key areas, who will use and live with the brand in the future. By integrating a vast number of respondents, we also wanted to inform and educate the general public about the importance of building the Slovenia brand.

The questionnaire comprised closed questions for proposed elements of brand identity as well as socio-demographic characteristics of the respondents. Questions were connected with six proposed elements of Slovenia's identity and were based on results gained from the Delphi study (Konecnik Ruzzier, 2011) and on reviews of relevant secondary data (Konecnik, 2004; Ministry of the Economy, 2007b; Musek, 1989, 1994; Šušteršič, Rojec, & Korenika, 2005). The questionnaire comprised two types of questions. In the first type the respondents were asked to evaluate their agreement or disagreement with claims about the most important elements of Slovenian identity on a 5-degree Likert scale (1 = least important, 5 = most important). The results are presented with means and standard deviations. Since our core aim was to present the opinions of key stakeholder groups about the main brand identity elements, the results are presented also by analysis of variance (F-test). Respondents were also asked to select what they regarded as the three most important answers concerning Slovenia brand identity elements. The results are presented with percentages. The SPSS tool was used to analyse the questionnaire.

4. Results of the quantitative research

Only fully completed questionnaires were used in the research, which included 707 respondents, of whom 60.4% were male and 39.6% female. Most respondents were aged from 26 to 35 years (38.9%), followed by the age group from 16 to 25 years (27.2%). Sixteen point four percent of respondents fell in the 36–45 age range, while a lesser percentage belonged to the age range of 46–55 (10.0%). Five point one percent respondents were aged between 56 and 65 years, followed by the respondents aged 66 years or more (1.7%). The smallest group represented respondents in the age 15 years or less (0.7%). Most respondents had secondary or high education (44.3%), followed by university education (39.6%). Twelve point seven percent of respondents had master or doctoral degree, followed by primary education (3.4%). Respondents were employed in six key country areas of employment: commerce (39.3%), tourism (18.4%), science (14.3%), state and civic matters (14.3%), culture and art (11.3%), and sport (2.4%).

4.1. Results about the most characteristic elements of I feel Slovenia identity

In the following part of the paper, we present the results concerning the most characteristic elements of Slovenia's brand identity. We follow the methodology of the I feel Slovenia identity model and present the elements as proposed in the first phase of the project (Konecnik Ruzzier & de Chernatony, in press): mission, vision, values, personality, distinguishing preferences, and benefits.

4.1.1. Mission and vision

Respondents' opinions about what characteristics they would like to see and experience in Slovenia in 10 years were quite unified. Preserved nature was mentioned as the most important characteristic among all key areas of employment (78.5%), followed by "Quality of life is more important than material prosperity" (49.2%), "Safe" (47.9%), "Preservation of Slovenian culture" (30.8%), and "Technological advancement" (26.2%).

The highest variation in opinions was noticed regarding technological advancement, which was chosen by 44.6% of respondents employed in science, compared to only 16.9% of respondents employed in tourism and 18.8% of respondents employed in politics and the civil service.

Regarding the vision Slovenia should follow, respondents evaluated the most important development policies for the country. Respondents stressed that Slovenia should become a country where modernity is combined with tradition without causing any environmental problems, and at the same time preserving Slovenian values and specialties (see Table 1). There were no significant differences among respondents from different employment areas regarding the stated development policy. Respondents on average agreed also that an important development policy for Slovenia is boutique entrepreneurship and micro-specialization in the sense of filling up market niches. With the analysis of variance we found that opinions about the second development policy varied among areas of employment ($p = 0.001$). The above-mentioned development policy was, on average, evaluated with the lowest rating by respondents employed in sports (mean = 3.35), compared to respondents employed in economy (mean = 3.85) and tourism (mean = 3.98), who evaluated this development policy with the highest rating.

From the above-presented results, we can conclude that respondents generally agreed with the Slovenia's mission. Furthermore, the results also show that respondents generally agreed with the vision Slovenia should follow in the future.

4.1.2. Values and personality

Respondents stressed that the most important characteristics of Slovenians are enthusiasm for the things they enjoy doing, diligence, active lifestyle, and orderliness. Respondents also agreed higher than the neutral mean with the attributes individuality and reserve as two of the important characteristics of Slovenians (see Table 2). Significant differences among respondents from different employment areas were evident in the evaluation of orderliness ($p = 0.04$) and low mobility ($p = 0.02$). Orderliness was on average evaluated higher by respondents employed in tourism (mean = 3.86) compared to those employed in

Table 1. The most desired development policies of Slovenia.

The most desired development policies of Slovenia	Mean	SD	Sig.
Slovenia should become a country where modernity is combined with tradition without causing any environmental problems and at the same time preserving Slovenian values and specialties	4.51	0.89	0.06
Slovenia should become a country with boutique entrepreneurship and micro-specialization in a sense of filling up market niches	3.74	1.17	**0.00***
Slovenia should become a role model for other countries regarding the incorporation process for the European Union and the transition to the new economic and social system	3.40	1.12	0.26

Note: $n = 707$; SD, standard deviation, *Significant at the 0.001 level.

Table 2. The most important characteristics of Slovenians.

The most important characteristics of Slovenians	Mean	SD	Sig.
Enthusiasm for the things they enjoy doing	4.09	0.98	0.56
Diligence	4.08	0.96	0.57
Active lifestyle	3.84	0.96	0.14
Orderliness	3.70	0.96	**0.04*****
Individualism	3.12	1.17	0.88
Reserve	2.90	1.17	0.16
Low mobility	2.86	1.29	**0.02*****
Cunning	2.66	1.12	0.31

Note: $n = 707$; SD, standard deviation, ***Significant at the 0.05 level.

science (mean = 3.47). We can conclude that respondents generally agreed what the traits of Slovenian personality and the main values are.

4.1.3. Physical features and distinguishing preferences

Mountains, the karst region and caves, forests, spas, Ljubljana, and autochthonous zoology and vegetation were evaluated as the most significant physical features of Slovenia (see Table 3). Significant differences among respondents from different areas of employment were evident in several stated features, including the Karst region and caves, forests, spas, the Pannonia plain, cities and villages, and the coast. The Karst and caves were on average evaluated higher by respondents employed in tourism (mean = 4.52) and culture and arts (mean = 4.50), compared to respondents employed in sports (mean = 3.82). Forests were on average evaluated higher by respondents employed in culture and arts (mean = 4.49) compared to respondents employed in sports (mean = 3.53). Furthermore, spas were on average evaluated higher by respondents employed in tourism (mean = 4.16) and on average lower by respondents employed in science (mean = 3.61).

Respondents pointed out green as the most typical colour of Slovenia (mean = 4.55). Respondents on average agreed that also blue (mean = 3.80), white (mean = 3.09), red (mean = 2.79), and yellow (mean = 2.52) represent typical Slovenian colours. Respondents did not associate black (mean = 1.40) and pink (mean = 1.29) colours with Slovenia. Respondents evaluated blue, white, red, orange, and pink similarly among all areas of employment. Differences in evaluation among respondents from diverse areas

Table 3. The most important physical features of Slovenia.

Slovenia's physical features	Mean	SD	Sig.
Mountains	4.44	0.77	0.31
Karst region and caves	4.42	0.82	**0.03*****
Forests	4.18	0.92	**0.00***
Spas	3.93	0.95	**0.00***
Ljubljana	3.61	1.21	0.36
Autochthonous zoology and vegetation	3.52	1.13	0.21
Pannonia plain	3.44	1.03	**0.00***
Cities and villages	3.38	1.11	**0.00***
Coast	3.27	1.12	0.05
Gardens and fields	2.86	1.06	**0.00***

Note: $n = 707$; SD, standard deviation, *Significant at the 0.001 level; ***Significant at the 0.005 level.

of employment were significant regarding yellow ($p = 0.00$), turquoise ($p = 0.01$), and black ($p = 0.00$).

Respondents on average agreed that they would describe Slovenia with the words: "Diversity in a small space." Respondents on average also agreed they would describe Slovenia with the following sentences: "Slovenians love the Slovene language but are aware of the great importance of communication skills in foreign languages."; "We are proud of Slovenia and its achievements."; "Slovenians are very hospitable."; "Slovenia is Europe in miniature."; and "Quality of life is at a high level." (see Table 4). Significant differences among respondents from different areas of employment were evident in the description: "Slovenians are very hospitable," which was on average evaluated the highest by respondents employed in tourism (mean = 3.82) compared to the lowest evaluation by respondents employed in science (mean = 3.33). Significant differences among respondents from different areas of employment were evident also with the description: "Slovenia is Europe in miniature," which was on average evaluated higher by tourism workers (mean = 3.70), compared to respondents employed in science (mean = 3.36) and sports (mean = 3.35). Furthermore, significant differences were also evident regarding the description "Slovenians are conscientious workers," which was evaluated higher by respondents employed in economy (mean = 3.67), compared to respondents employed in culture and arts (mean = 3.28) and tourism (mean = 3.34).

Respondents believed that the diversity of landscapes is Slovenia's most important distinguishing feature (see Table 5). Nature conservation, safety, orderliness, and authenticity were on average also evaluated as important distinguishing features of Slovenia. Significant differences were evident among the classification of Slovenian language and its grammatical features, which were on average evaluated higher by respondents from culture and arts (mean = 3.73), compared to respondents employed in politics and the civil service (mean = 3.03), tourism (mean = 3.11), and economy (mean = 3.24). Significant differences were evident also among the evaluation of niche orientation, which was on average evaluated higher by respondents employed in tourism (mean = 3.43) and economy (mean = 3.17), compared to respondents employed in science (mean = 2.81).

Table 4.   Slovenia's description for foreigners.

Slovenia's description for foreigners	Mean	SD	Sig.
Diversity in a small space	4.66	0.70	0.60
Slovenians love the Slovene language but are aware of the great importance of communication skills in foreign languages	3.84	1.13	0.54
We are proud of Slovenia and its achievements	3.64	1.17	0.65
Slovenians are very hospitable	3.57	1.03	**0.01****
Slovenia is Europe in miniature	3.51	1.26	**0.04*****
Quality of life is at a high level	3.51	1.04	0.19
Slovenians are conscientious workers	3.50	1.07	**0.01****
Slovenia is famous for its tidiness	3.33	0.98	0.69
Every Slovenian is working extra after work	3.17	1.21	0.15
Slovenians will passionately participate in a debate, but eventually welcome the agreement	2.68	1.11	0.63

Note: $n = 707$; SD, standard deviation, **Significant at 0.01 level. ***Significant at 0.05 level.

Table 5. Distinguishing features of Slovenia.

Distinguishing features of Slovenia	Mean	SD	Sig.
The diversity of landscapes	4.54	0.83	0.45
Nature conservation	4.34	0.81	0.16
Safety	4.11	0.93	0.07
Orderliness	3.72	1.01	0.84
Authenticity	3.62	1.07	0.15
Slovenian language and its grammatical features	3.26	1.30	**0.01**
Strong belonging to the hometown	3.25	1.30	0.50
Niche orientation	3.17	1.06	**0.00***

Note: $n = 707$; SD, standard deviation, *Significant at 0.001 level; **Significant at 0.01 level.

The three most important dualities were chosen from respondents in all areas of employment. The most characteristic duality: "Diversity (regional, climatic, cultural) – Ethnic homogeneity (most citizens are Slovenians)," was chosen by as many as 72.4% of respondents, followed by "Young country (from 1991) – Long history," (59.4%) and "Travellers – Not migrant" (59%). Only respondents employed in culture and arts also chose among the most important dualities "Mediterranean self-indulgence – Northern pedantry".

From the above-stated opinions we can conclude that respondents generally agreed about the most characteristic physical features and distinguishing preferences of Slovenia. Respondents emphasized preserved nature, diversity of landscapes, Slovene language, safety, and ethnic homogeneity among the main distinguishing preferences.

4.1.4. Benefits

Respondents also evaluated which benefits would attract foreigners to Slovenia. Seventy-six percent chose unspoilt nature as the most influential benefit, followed by quality of life (52.8%), diverse options for leisure activities (52.3%), and accessible location for vacation (40.5%). Respondents from diverse areas of employment were unified in their evaluation of unspoilt nature as the most influential benefit. While most of the respondents put quality of life in the top three positions, respondents employed in sports evaluated quality of life as only the fifth most important benefit (35.3%). Respondents employed in sports stressed diverse options for leisure activities (52.9%) and sports activities and quality of workforce (both 41.2%). From the above-stated results, we can conclude that respondents generally agreed about the main benefits of Slovenia.

4.1.5. Summary of the results

The results of the quantitative research show similar views concerning the identity of Slovenia. Deviations regarding elements of Slovenian identity can be explained by the peculiarities of each area (arts and culture emphasize cultural traits, tourism relies on hospitality, etc.). On the basis of the presented results we can conclude that Slovenians share a common opinion about Slovenian identity elements.

Contrary to the findings of this research, earlier studies of Slovenia brand development and the formation of country characteristics were unable to find a united opinion or agreement on the characteristics of the Slovenia brand. Additional reasons why we did not detect significant differences in the perception of important elements of the Slovenia brand among respondents are presented further.

The integrated approach used in the process of the I feel Slovenia brand development, which included a wide variety of key stakeholder groups, seems like a sound approach when building a country brand. By integrating diverse stakeholders, their opinions can be gained fundamentally and later appropriately adjusted and coordinated. The chosen methodological approach provided the basis for the adoption of diverse opinions and directed the debate concerning the gradual harmonization of opinions about brand identity among diverse stakeholder groups. The good side of such a methodological approach is its impartiality and the gradual approximation to the identity agreed upon by the majority of participants. The disadvantage of this approach lies in the fact that certain powerful elements lose their sharpness when a certain group distinctively disagrees with chosen elements. Moreover, although we assumed that severe variations would be evident due to earlier attempts of Slovenia brand formation, later we did not detect strong disagreements among diverse stakeholder groups. The research results, which confirm the high degree of agreement among the participants in the process of Slovenia brand development, suggest that Slovenes generally agree with the main features of Slovenia, Slovenians, and the desired traits for the future.

Nevertheless, the limitation of this research should also be highlighted, which is the inclusion of the non-probability sample among stakeholder groups. Furthermore, key areas of the country have been designed according to the subsequent implementation of the brand and, therefore, do not correspond with the current categorization of activities in Slovenia. An approximate number of representatives from the key areas were invited to participate in the process, which roughly matches the number of employees in key areas. Moreover, prevailing opinions were taken into account regardless of the number of respondents in each stakeholder group. Although this is not the probability sample, the research results imply that the opinions obtained are, to a large extent, common to all key internal stakeholder groups in the country. Therefore, the results present an outstanding starting point for the current brand and allow it the possibility of developing into a successful and strong brand which will clearly position Slovenia on the world map.

5. Conclusion and implications

Country brand management and marketing are regarded as more complex than management of other brand types, since many internal and external stakeholders should be considered. Recent scientific contributions highlight the great importance of identification with the brand by internal stakeholders who will actively experience the brand and live with it in the future (de Chernatony, 1999; Konecnik & Go, 2008; Konecnik Ruzzier & Ruzzier, 2009; Morgan & Pritchard, 2002). Therefore, it is very important to include diverse internal stakeholder groups already in the process of brand development and thus make it possible to actively co-create the brand they will be living with in the future (Konecnik Ruzzier, 2011).

The paper presents the steps in the process of developing the identity of the I feel Slovenia brand. The process was systematic and integrated since representatives of key country areas were invited to take part in the process. A systematic process consequently led to the elements of brand identity agreed by the vast majority of stakeholders. In the main part of the paper, we focus on quantitative research among representatives from key country areas. Research results indicate the high degree of consensus among participants. Respondents clearly highlighted the most important characteristics of the Slovenia brand, which are related to nature and the Slovenian green colour and are reflected in all elements of the brand's identity. We can, therefore, assume that Slovenes generally agree about the main identity characteristics of Slovenia, merged in the new brand I feel Slovenia.

As stressed in the paper, the respondents' opinions from the quantitative research presented a basis for the Slovenia brand development. Gained general opinions from diverse stakeholder groups were incorporated into the proposed brand identity model. Results of the whole process are the brand identity elements presented below. According to respondents' opinions, Slovenia's mission is captured within the statement: "Forward with nature." Also vision reflects respondents' opinions while emphasizing green boutiqueness and organic development. Highlighted values of Slovenia are family, health, and responsibility. Brand personality traits include enthusiasm for the things Slovenians enjoy doing, diligence, active lifestyle, individualism, and a wish for recognition. Benefits encourage activity, quality of life, and being in touch with nature. Distinguishing preferences of Slovenia are the proximity of differences, safety, Slovene language and its dialects, and preserved natural environment. Furthermore, the Slovenian identity is presented with the story which emphasizes common Slovenian characteristics. Later on the main story is adapted to all highlighted key areas, where emphasized elements on each key area represent the distinguishing characteristics of individual area. Nevertheless the main message of the I feel Slovenia brand is that Slovenia should be experienced, since images cannot illustrate the whole Slovenian experience (Ministry of the Economy, 2007a).

A vast number of scientists and practitioners emphasize that only strong country brands with incisive story and unique identity will succeed on the market and consequently attract highly desired tourists, investors, and support the export of domestic goods and services (Fan, 2006; Moilanen, 2007; Morgan et al., 2003). However, the success of the country brand does not depend just on the development of the unique brand with distinctive identity. Even though brand identity elements gathered from opinions of representatives of various internal stakeholder groups present a strong basis for the I feel Slovenia brand, systematic work and consistency in communicating the identity to a variety of internal and external stakeholders are needed for the brand's success in the long run. Finally, as emphasized in the literature, identification of the internal stakeholders with the brands' identity will be crucial for its long-term success and survival. Therefore, we believe that the inclusion of internal stakeholders into the brand development process as presented in the paper is crucial for every country brands' success.

References

Bieger, T. (2000). *Management von Destinationen und Tourismusorganisationen*. Muenchen: Oldenbourg.

Buhalis, D. (2000). Marketing the competitive destination of the future. *Tourism Management, 21*, 97–116.

Cai, L.A. (2002). Cooperative branding for rural destinations. *Annals of Tourism Research, 29*, 720–742.

de Chernatony, L. (1999). Brand management through narrowing the gap between brand identity and brand reputation. *Journal of Marketing Management, 15*, 157–179.

de Chernatony, L. (2010). *From brand vision to brand evaluation*. Oxford: Butterworth-Heinemann.

de Chernatony, L., & Dall'Olmo Riley, F. (1999). Experts' views about defining service brands and the principles of services branding. *Journal of Business Research, 46*, 181–192.

Dinnie, K. (2004). Place branding: An overview of an emerging literature. *Place Branding and Public Diplomacy, 1*, 106–110.

Dinnie, K. (2008). *Nation branding: Concepts, issues, practice*. Oxford: Butterworth-Heinemann.

Fan, Y. (2006). Branding the nation: What is being branded? *Journal of Vacation Marketing, 12*, 5–14.

Hankinson, G. (2007). The management of destination brands: Five guiding principles based on recent developments in corporate branding theory. *Journal of Brand Management, 14*, 240–254.

Hanna, S., & Rowley, J. (2008). An analysis of terminology use in place branding. *Place Branding and Public Diplomacy, 4*, 61–75.

Kavaratzis, M. (2005). Place branding: A review of trends and conceptual models. *The Marketing Review, 5*, 329–342.

Konecnik, M. (2004). Evaluating Slovenia's image as a tourism destination: A self analysis process towards building a destination brand. *Journal of Brand Management, 11*, 307–316.

Konecnik, M., & Gartner, W.C. (2007). Customer-based brand equity for a destination. *Annals of Tourism Research, 34*, 400–421.

Konecnik, M., & Go, F. (2008). Tourism destination brand identity: The case of Slovenia. *Journal of Brand Management, 15*, 177–189.

Konecnik Ruzzier, M. (2009). Notranji pogled na razvoj znamke I feel Slovenia: Soustvarjanje njene identitete s pomočjo mnenj strokovnjakov. *Organizacija, 42*, A188–A193, Retrieved from http://organizacija.fov.uni-mb.si/index.php/organizacija-en/article/viewFile/1018/857.

Konecnik Ruzzier, M. (2011). Country brand and identity issues: Slovenia. In N. Morgan, A. Pritchard, & R. Pride (Eds.), *Destination brands: Managing place reputation* (pp. 291–302). Oxford: Butterworth-Heinemann.

Konecnik Ruzzier, M., & de Chernatony, L. (in press). Developing and applying a place brand identity model: The case of Slovenia. *Journal of Business Research.*

Konecnik Ruzzier, M., Lapajne, P., Drapal, A., & de Chernatony, L. (2009). Celostni pristop k oblikovanju identitete znamke I feel Slovenia. *Akademija MM, 9*(13), 51–62, Retrieved from http://www.dlib.si/details/URN:NBN:SI:DOC-VY2NSFT8/?query=%27 keywords%3 dakademija+MM%27&pageSize=20.

Konecnik Ruzzier, M., & Ruzzier, M. (2009). A two-dimensional approach to branding: Integrating identity and equity. In L.A. Cai, W.C. Gartner, & A.M. Munar (Eds.), *Tourism branding: Communities in action* (pp. 65–73). Bingley: Emerald.

Ministry of the Economy (2007a). The brand of Slovenia., Retrieved from http://www.majakonecni k.com/konecnik/dokumenti/File/brandbook_ifeelslovenia.pdf.

Ministry of the Economy (2007b). Development plan and policies for Slovene tourism 2007–2011., Retrieved from http://www.mg.gov.si/fileadmin/mg.gov.si/pageuploads/razpisi/JN/DT/publi kacija_RNUST_ang_SPLET.pdf.

Moilanen, T. (2007). Building a country brand., Retrieved from http://www.mek.fi/w5/mekfi/index. nsf/730493a8cd104eacc4322570ac00411b4b/6d8dff0ecdf09be9c22573540028b6eb/$FILE/ Teemu_Moilanen_280807engl.ppt.

Morgan, N., & Pritchard, A. (2002). Contextualizing destination branding. In N. Morgan, A. Pritchard, & R. Pride (Eds.), *Destination branding: Creating the unique destination proposition* (pp. 10–41). Oxford: Butterworth-Heinemann.

Morgan, N., Pritchard, A., & Piggott, R. (2002). New Zealand, 100% pure. The creation of a powerful niche destination brand. *Journal of Brand Management, 9*, 335–354.

Morgan, N.J., Pritchard, A., & Piggott, R. (2003). Destination branding and the role of the stakeholders: The case of New Zealand. *Journal of Vacation Marketing, 9*, 285–299.

Musek, J. (1989). O osebnostnem profilu Slovencev. *Anthropos, 20*(1–2), 270–286, Retrieved from http://www.anthropos.si/kaj.html.

Musek, J. (1994). *Osebnostni portret Slovencev.* Ljubljana: Znanstveno in publicistično središče.

O'Shaughnessy, J., & O'Shaughnessy, N.J. (2000). Treating the nation as a brand: Some neglected issues. *Journal of Macromarketing, 20*, 56–64.

Pike, S. (2005). Tourism destination branding complexity. *Journal of Product and Brand Management, 14*, 258–259.

Pike, S. (2009). Destination brand positions of a competitive set of near-home destinations. *Tourism Management, 60*, 857–866.

Ryan, C. (2002). The politics of branding cities and regions: The case of New Zealand. In N. Morgan, A. Pritchard, & R. Pride (Eds.), *Destination branding: Creating the unique destination proposition* (pp. 66–86). Oxford: Butterworth-Heinemann.

Šušteršič, J., Rojec, M., & Korenika, K. (2005). *Strategija razvoja Slovenije.* Ljubljana: Urad Republike Slovenije za makroekonomske analize in razvoj.

Unpacking the temporal dimension of coopetition in tourism destinations: evidence from Finnish and Italian theme parks

Mika Kylanen[a] and Marcello M. Mariani[b]

[a]School of Tourism and Hospitality Management, Lapland Institute for Tourism Research and Education, Rovaniemi University of Applied Sciences, Viirinkankaantie, 1, FI-96101 Rovaniemi, Finland; [b]Dipartimento di Scienze Aziendali, University of Bologna, Via Capo di Lucca, 34, IT-40126 Bologna, Italy

Coopetition, namely the co-presence of cooperation and competition, is a new strategy that goes beyond the established business paradigms of competition and cooperation. This type of strategy is relevant in tourism destinations, for instance in theme parks, where competing, co-located companies also collaborate. In this paper, we address the temporal dynamics of interorganizational relationships in Finnish and Italian theme parks (i.e. Lapland and Riviera Romagnola). Our comparative study shows that cooperation and coopetition among tourism businesses often shift from a prevalently short-term basis to a long term one when public and private stakeholders understand the benefits accruing to cooperation in terms of enhancement of the brand image of the destination and attraction of a higher number of visitors, by leveraging the destination's multifaceted assets.

1. Introduction

In the field of management, marketing, and tourism studies, the two leading paradigms of competition and cooperation have recently been juxtaposed to a novel situation referred to as coopetition (Bengtsson & Kock, 2000; Dagnino & Rocco, 2009; Mariani, 2007). This stands for simultaneous cooperation and competition (Dagnino & Rocco, 2009; Mariani, 2007, 2008). Tourism destinations offer a fertile context to study coopetition (Kylänen & Rusko, 2011). In fact, tourism destinations mirror the changes and challenges of complex globalized business environments, wherein interorganizational relationships and dynamics are acquiring more and more importance over time, especially in order to increase the value of a destination for potential tourists. For instance, cooperation may come into picture when originally competing, co-located companies want to render their destination more attractive among stakeholders and potential customers and tourists. However, to shift between competition, cooperation, and coopetition, seems not an easy, clear-cut call or an intentional and rational strategic decision, but more contextual and complex processes. It can take indeed an emergent, unintentional, and socio-cultural form (Kylänen & Rusko, 2011; Mariani, 2007, 2008, 2009).

The purpose of our paper is to characterize the temporal dynamics of coordination between spatially competing co-located actors. In particular, we highlight when, why, and how temporal dimensions modify competitive and cooperative attitudes and behaviour, and their simultaneous presence, namely coopetitive interorganizational relationships. Temporality in coopetition refers to timing, rhythm, and decision time frame of business identity creation and business practices.

Coopetition and its coordination from a socio-cultural perspective are largely under-explored and often confined to an impenetrable black box (Mariani, 2007). Our study tries to bridge this gap and builds on the idea that strategic thinking and action should not be addressed only from a rational-managerial perspective but rather from a socio-cultural perspective where also other actors, directions, approaches, and motives should be taken in consideration. In particular, our perspective is both process based and institutional. Indeed, in addition to a micro-level analysis (e.g. decision-making processes leading to coopetition), we also make visible the institutional environment (e.g. a public authorities dictating major changes) in order to discuss the formation of competitive, cooperative, and/or coopetitive arrangements, and the actual underlying processes and practices through which they are maintained, discontinued, or resumed.

We situate our ongoing empirical analysis in two European tourism destinations, i.e. industrial districts that are geographically circumscribed, where businesses tend to cooperate in the medium-long term in order to achieve a successful long-term destination branding strategy while they compete on a shorter term for the hearts, minds, and wallets of the customers.

More specifically, we have explored the development of cooperative and coopetitive ventures among a relevant number of businesses in two destinations – namely the Lapland (Finland) on one hand and the Riviera di Romagna (Italy) on the other – over a long span of time (7 years).

The paper is structured as follows. In Section 2, we illustrate our theoretical background which is mainly interdisciplinary as it builds on three different research streams: (1) coopetition strategies, (2) interorganizational relationships, and (3) tourism destination management. In Section 3, we clarify our epistemological perspective, describe the empirical setting (i.e. the two destinations/areas under comparison), and exemplify the methods and techniques used for fieldwork. Section 4 describes our business cases. Section 5 provides a comparative discussion of our cases and findings, relating them to cooperation and coopetition and their temporal dimensions. Section 6 includes several conclusions and major implications for academicians, business practitioners, and policy-makers. This last section offers several reflections about the limitations of our study and illustrates a future itinerary of coopetitive research in the tourism industry.

2. Literature review

Our theoretical framework builds on three different research streams: (1) coopetition strategies, (2) interorganizational relationships, and (3) tourism destination management. The recent stream of coopetition strategy literature has emphasized that in many practical cases organizations tend to both compete and cooperate simultaneously, thus generating an apparently new form of interorganizational dynamic named coopetition (Brandenburger & Nalebuff, 1996; Brandenburger & Stuart, 1996). So far, this new interorganizational dynamic has been analysed from a theoretical point of view (Gnyawali & Madhavan, 2001; Lado, Boyd, & Hanlon, 1997); nonetheless, empirical research is still scant (Luo, 2005), but see also the 2007 Special Issue on Coopetition Strategy in *International Studies in Management and Organization* and a recent anthology on coopetition published by Dagnino & Rocco (2009). In particular, the emphasis has been more on the level of outcomes and deterministic strategies, whereas the actual processes (how) and antecedents (why) of coopetition have remained uncovered (Kylänen & Rusko, 2011; Mariani, 2007, 2009).

Management scholars dealing with interorganizational relationships have analysed several features of strategies within strategic alliances and collectives of organizations (Astley, 1984; Astley & Fombrun, 1983). As much as the former ones are concerned, organizations have been depicted as actors relying on cooperative devices in order to achieve a superior competitive advantage (e.g. Contractor & Lorange, 1988; Garcia-Canal, Duarte, Criado, & Llaneza, 2002; Hakansson & Snehota, 1995; Lavie, 2006; Powell, Koput, & Smith-Doerr, 1996; Zaheer, 1995). As far as the latter ones are concerned, organizations have been portrayed as members of a collective, jointly mobilizing action and resources towards the achievement of shared ends (e.g. Astley, 1984; Barnett, Mischke, & Ocasio, 2000; Bresser, 1988; Dacin, Oliver, & Roy, 2007; Reur & Ariño, 2007).

Tourism destinations, their evolution, and destination management offer a fertile context to study coopetition. Tourism destinations mirror the changes and challenges of complex globalized business environments in many ways. As Van Laere and Heene (2003) point out, globalization does not only make competition fiercer, but also cooperation becomes more intense when companies, regions, and networks search to keep up with the pace and nature of change and especially when co-located tourism companies want to render the destination they belong to more attractive than other ones. As a consequence, it seems that a shift from a competitive paradigm to a more collaborative approach to tourism business is taking place (Fyall & Garrod, 2005; Wang, 2008; Wang & Krakover, 2007).

Since tourism products deal with meanings and interplay of production cultures, consumption cultures, and local cultures (García-Rosell, Haanpää, Kylänen, & Markuksela, 2007), it is possible to identify a further major change from mass production to more flexible post-Fordist production principles. These changes also indicate some specialties of tourism production and consumption. Firstly, it can be said that the success and contents of tourism products stem from socio-cultural features of a place as tourism often deals with locations that have put their locality, culture, and community on the frame. This emphasizes the powerful social impact, but also the delicate nature of tourism (e.g. Higgins-Desbiolles, 2006).

Secondly, since tourism destinations can be considered as business agglomerations and industrial districts (see Becattini, 2002; Hjalager, 2000; Staber, 1998), the co-location, proximity, and interconnectedness of global and local tourism companies of different size create possibilities for businesses to cooperate, but also to compete. Interconnectedness of tourism is evident in supply chains and networks that take place on both regional–national and national–international level. In fact, tourism destination dynamics make visible the simultaneity of cooperation and competition (see also, for example, Lado et al., 1997).

The third, and probably the most decisive, specialty of tourism (compared to many other businesses) is its unique product. Indeed, tourists experience the destination holistically as a seamless entirety consisting of many different products provided by both private and public organizations. Hence, tourists rarely enter and experience the destination for and with one company only. Although visiting a certain firm and buying services from separate companies, the customer connects oneself to the destination as a whole (see, for example, Stamboulis & Skayannis, 2003; von Friedrichs Grängsjö, 2001).

3. Methodology

An in-depth qualitative approach has been adopted in the present study due to its consistency with our exploratory and descriptive aim (Eisenhardt, 1989; Glaser & Strauss, 1967; Miles & Huberman, 1984; Strauss, 1987). Our research design includes a vast amount of data gathered systematically during 7 years. It covers in total almost 10 business cases on two tourism destination areas of Lapland, Finland, and Riviera Romagnola, Italy. Our analysis is based on a longitudinal perspective (Pettigrew, 1990) and observation (Hammersley & Atkinson, 1995). The case study approach is preferable to other research methodologies (experiments, questionnaires, etc.) when (a) we know little about a phenomenon and current perspectives seem inadequate since they have little empirical substantiation (see Eisenhardt, 1989) and (b) we intend to answer to questions related to "why" and "how" of certain aspects or phenomena (see Eriksson & Kovalainen, 2008).

3.1. *Presentation of the cases*

More specifically, the cases analysed in the study are the Santa Claus Village (FIN1) in Lapland, Finland, and Aquafan, Mirabilandia theme parks (ITA1) in Romagna region. Particularly, we have benefited from a versatile set of qualitative methodologies ranging from case studies to ethnographic fieldwork and action research. We have used thematic and semi-structured interviews, company visits, participatory and non-participant observation, workshops, and document data in the two sites to gain a more thorough view of the ways coopetition gets understood, accounted for and acted upon (see, for example, Hammersley & Atkinson, 1995; Nason & Golding, 1998; van Maanen, 1979). A more thorough presentation of the studied sites and their local/global connections will be provided below (see also http://www.santaclausvillage.info, http://www.visitrovaniemi.fi, and http://www.rivieraromagnola.net).

The cases are structured in such a way that they highlight the following items: (1) the *history* of the business/resort/destination/theme park/site; (2) the overall *structure* of the business (e.g. organizational features) and how it relates to relevant stakeholders such as destination management organizations (DMOs) and to other businesses through networks or dyadic relationships; (3) the description of the formation and development of interorganizational and *cooperative and coopetitive dynamics* between selected companies, with a focus on practices and motives, as well as on the institutional environment.

3.2. *Interviews*

In Italy, semi-structured interviews have been conducted with key personnel, e.g. the top management, middle management, and officials, of the chosen destinations and/or companies (for a total of seven interviewees). In Lapland, thematic interviews have been conducted with key personnel, e.g. entrepreneurs/owners and managers of tourism companies and tourism associations in the chosen destinations. Altogether, in Lapland, there were five interviewees from the Santa Claus Village and two interviewees from the Rovaniemi Tourism & Marketing Ltd (a regional association). The interviews lasted from 30 min up to 2 h. Mainly, thematic structure was followed in the interviews covering the topics with a range encompassing from company-level information to the levels of regional and international cooperation. Also, structural, attitudinal, and historical differences that create challenges and tensions to competition and cooperation were discussed in the interviews. In particular, operational rhythm, strategic/tactical/operational time frame and decision-making processes were in the foci of the business interviews. The interviewees were asked to describe and evaluate their business practices and their connection to entrepreneurial identity processes. The particular motive for conducting interviews, and thus, paying attention to the voice of the entrepreneurs, was to learn about what kind of meanings the interviewees give to strategic and operational plans and actions related to them.

3.3. Archival data

With regard to the archival sources, published information and sector studies released by the Tourism authorities such as the Assessorati al Turismo, Regional Council of Lapland, and tourism associations of relevant regions, provinces and municipalities were examined (e.g. the report of APT Emilia Romagna), as well as press releases, leaflets, pamphlets, and materials generated by consortia management and tourism policy-makers. Detailed information about operations was found also in the organizations' annual reports. The role of document data was to enrich the other forms of data acquisition, but also to bridge the gap between saying and doing. For instance, when discussing cooperation in marketing activities it is equally interesting to see whether the marketing material used is in line with the notions made by the interviewee. An additionally interesting angle was to analyze what is said in the brochures etc., and what is left uncovered.

3.4. Observations

Both in Finland and in Italy, ethnographic fieldwork also played an important role in the overall data sample. In particular, participant and non-participant on-site observation has taken place in the destinations under study. Observation has taken place in about 20 official and unofficial meetings and events, product testing occasions, and customer encounters. For instance, the meetings have included get-togethers with local companies, municipalities, governmental organizations, and other stakeholders. The meetings have lasted from 20 min up to 4 h covering planning and decision-making in the areas of product development, marketing, cooperation and strategic management, and also administrative issues. Together with the interviews and the document data, this fieldwork data form a diverse and thorough set of information for an in-depth analysis. The particular motive in using the observation method was to find out how things take place in natural settings. Observation method has been useful for us, since we have studied socially organized groups and institutional surroundings with specific work practices, values and relationships with our aim to identify and understand meanings, concrete processes and the aforementioned saying/doing gap *in situ* (see, for example, Hammersley & Atkinson, 1995). For instance, observation was important in covering the concrete processes, practices, rhythm, and atmosphere of coopetitive development work.

4. Cases

4.1. Santa Claus Village, Rovaniemi

The Santa Claus Village is a tourism attraction located in the outskirts of the city of Rovaniemi, in Lapland, Finland. It is one of the premier tourism attractions in Northern Europe (Pretes, 2007). It is a shopping village complex that also includes several activity services, restaurants, souvenir and craftsman shops, accommodation, and sites to visit and experience. This agglomeration of small business (tens of souvenir shops, programme service companies, art and activities around snow and ice, other types of sites, and cafes and restaurants) has a more or less unified theme related to Santa Claus and Christmas, and it invites about 250,000 tourists per year. The most interesting site in the village is Santa Claus Office where people can visit the Santa Claus every day and take a group photo with him; Santa Claus Post Office that receives hundreds of thousands of letters to Santa from all around the world; Christmas House that hosts an exhibition about international Christmas traditions; and shopping departments that sell Finnish design clothes and materials of Marimekko, and glass art and kitchen utensils of Iittala. More recently, the concept has been extended to include Santa Park, Santa Claus' home cave that is a children- and family-oriented theme park. Also, there are some husky and reindeer enclosures situated nearby.

The history of the village begins in year 1950 when the First Lady Eleanor Roosevelt wanted to visit Rovaniemi to see the progress of the post-war reconstruction work. The city officials wanted to build a tourism attraction where to take her, so a traditional Northern Finnish cabin was built by the highway leading to north. Even before the war, there used to be a pole to mark the Arctic Circle as a geographical landmark.

The development of Christmas- and Santa Claus-related tourism in Lapland dates back to the 1980s. The Finnish Tourism Board was willing to promote Finland's and Lapland's tourism image by creating a new marketing programme. A specific focus was put on the theme of Christmas and Santa Claus as a tourism attraction. In 1984, the Governor of Lapland declared the province "Santa Claus Land", and initiated the development of several Christmas-themed attractions. The Santa Claus Village was opened in 1985. Today, charter jets from the UK and elsewhere in Europe bring visitors for short-term package tours, allowing them to experience not only the Santa Claus Village attractions themselves, but also reindeer-drawn sledge rides, Sámi culture, and the snowy scenery of Lapland. In addition to international tour operators, individual tourists arrive by plane, but also the Meetings, Incentive, Convention and Events (MICE) segment is constantly growing in importance (Pretes, 2007).

The companies working in the area have organized their joint activities under an entrepreneurs' association to pool resources in planning and marketing and to complement each other for a Christmas-related customer experience. The Santa Claus Village has many advantages in the light of current and emerging tourism trends; theme-based tourism and endless possibilities in product development around Christmas and Santa Claus, and Christmas ideology with its good values appeals to people around the world with its universal story. However, the companies have proved to be rather arguing, and only recently the over-commercialism has become challenged by authentic multi-sensory Christmas experiences where the good values have also been connected to business values (see Kylänen, 2007; Pretes, 1995, 2007).

> I have tried to convince my fellow entrepreneurs in the association, and the city and province officials, too, to shift from mass tourism to more authentic experiences. Our product, the village, should be less about commercialism and materialism, and more about pure values of Christmas. Today, the customers search for meanings and experiences, and we have the possibility to "tackle" that ... However, this calls for cooperation and mutual understanding (Interviewee #5).

The role of the Santa Claus Village for the city of Rovaniemi and its gateway position for Lapland tourism is very important. However, cooperative and competitive tensions between the village and the city centre without forgetting the cooperation–competition imbalance within the village, among the entrepreneurs, are under constant debate. For instance, in the village a cottage village providing accommodation services has been opened for this summer season, and this may cause a situation where the tourists cannot or do not have to visit the city centre at all during their short visit. Also, disagreements between some key entrepreneurs in the village and the similarity of the (souvenir) products have hindered the possibilities of inter-firm cooperation.

> Well, the [entrepreneurs'] association is not too active, you know, but of course, I should have been more active myself, too. Anyway, we have had some quarrels within the village, but I think the situation has got much better now. Especially the role of the city officials and developers has been central. They have helped us to see beyond our short-sighted competitive spirit, and have made efforts towards more cooperative attitude in the village, among the company representatives, I mean (Interviewee #3).

As described by an entrepreneur, the role of the municipality and the public officials has been important to initiate and maintain cooperative atmosphere in the village. This has become even more emphasized for a brand development project where the city officials together with local entrepreneurs and researchers and developers have co-created an "experience lab" where the business, the public sector, the research and development, and even the customers can meet and develop things together (LEO Finland, 2010). In the following years, this will also clear the way for a more systematic strategic planning, even a strategy document, for the village and/or destination (Rovaniemi).

The village is under constant development work. In the following years, more emphasis will be put on unified quality standards (e.g. "made in china" vs. local handicrafts), visual image and marketing, extension of the key product (from Santa as a site/person to visit vs. good values and meanings attached to Christmas time more generally to invite more companies beyond Santa figure), and more thorough and broad-minded, year-round Christmas branding of Rovaniemi (with an important angle based on the village). It seems to be widely acknowledged that Christmas-related product should lean more heavily on holistic meaningful experiences around the year than simple gift-giving during Christmas time.

Obviously, the relationship and balance between cooperation and competition is an important issue to follow, if not to solve. If the village is to shift from a single attraction ("a one-trick-pony", "once-in-a-life-time", such as to pay a visit to the Santa Claus) to a more diverse and durable experience, the product should be more augmented. This calls for a more cooperative approach be it a direction towards self-supporting, thematic village attraction or a more Rovaniemi-driven destination product. Along the same vein, involvement of the local people and creation of a more unified destination "metascript", a philosophy for the site, are the next important steps to the village development. As indicated in the quote below, companies seem to struggle from day to day with their entrepreneurship spirit where they focus on themselves compared to their altruism and cooperative spirit where they think about their business more broadly.

> For us, companies, it is not always the easiest of tasks to look outside our windows and doors. As an entrepreneur you have to concentrate mainly on yourself, isn't it so. However, this village is our joint product, and we all have our role to play in it. We have to learn to think about our customers to make them come, and the entire village to develop the destination as a whole. Sometimes, in the development projects you may face a situation where every company can't win at the same time. Some of them may benefit in the short-run while others may have to wait a lil' longer (Interviewee #2).

This can be identified as contrasting attitudes and forms of behaviour of "company first" versus "destination first" (von Friedrichs Grängsjö, 2003). To balance the coopetitive values, norms, and behaviour in the Santa Claus Village, and to serve both the company and the destination interests, we seem to need both economic-rational and value-emotional attachment by the company representatives towards the destination.

4.2. The theme parks in the Riviera Romagnola: a focus on Mirabilandia

Many of the most popular Italian theme parks are located in the Riviera di Romagna area. More specifically the list includes the following: Mirabilandia, Aquafan, Oltremare, Italia in Miniatura, Fiabilandia. In what follows, for convenience sake, we have concentrated our attention on Mirabilandia business case and then have related this case with the one of its direct competitors (Aquafan).

Mirabilandia is today one of the most important theme parks in Italy, with an average number of 2 million visitors per year over the last 5 years. The history of Mirablinadia can be broken down in three phases. In 1987, the company "Parco della Standiana" was created by Finbrescia (46%), San Paolo Finance (44%) and Publitalia (10%), with a total investment of 150 billion Liras. The park was opened in July 1992, with expectation of 1 million visitors. Nonetheless, during the first 5 years of activity, the park recorded low levels of visitors (till in 1996 it had only 660,000 visitors) due to significant mistakes in forecasting, managerial inexperience, and harsh competition with the direct competitors in the Riviera Romagnola (Aquafan). This first stage of the history of Mirabilandia was concluded with Mirabilandia filing for bankruptcy.

The second stage of development registers the new property Loeffelhardt/Casoli taking over in 1997. Starting from this moment, a multi-annual plan for massive investment was set up including (1) new giant rides and shows, also borrowed from the partner park Phantasialand; (2) new logo and mascot; (3) TV appearances; and (4) an effort to compete less and to cooperate more with other theme parks in the territory (particularly with Aquafan). This stage ends in 2003 with the opening of Mirabilandia Beach Water Park.

The third stage starts with the acquisition of the park by the Spanish group Parques Reunidos in 2006. In 2007, Parques Reunidos is bought by the British investment fund Candover. This fund managed to provide a great contribution of expertise and funds for important new attractions such as Reset and iSpeed, but without changing the structure of the management and creative team (artists, craftsmen, technicians, etc.) which are entirely Italian.

If we look at the breakdown of visitors of Mirabilandia, a clear trend shows up: visitors who chose Mirabilandia as a destination increase over time more than visitors who visited Mirabilandia just because they were visiting The Riviera di Romagna or because they are local residents.

This state of affairs is common also for the other theme parks of the Riviera di Romagna (e.g. Aquafan) and points to the fact that all of the theme parks under consideration should be conceived as a set of destinations with similar (but not identical) features, able to attract visitors and tourists by themselves, regardless of the fact that their tourists are interested specifically in the Riviera di Romagna. This was understood by the managers of the most relevant parks in the late 90s and led to a number of cooperative initiatives that took place especially during the last decade starting from 2000. These initiatives relate to different forms of cooperation for the promotion of the theme parks themselves. As one of the top managers underlined:

> We want that before leaving to Riviera they [the visitors of Romagna] should know that they have a variety of choices in terms of theme parks and we hope of course to be "THE" choice for them. But if we don't collaborate to build an image of Riviera as a region rich with theme parks, then we might have less visitors, so cooperation is very important (Interviewee #2).

Moreover, it is clear from several interviews that in the late 90s every and each of the managers started looking at the other theme parks as coopetitors serving the same destination with a diversified offer of entertainment activities so that:

> We are complementary and my park has something different from the others and it's the same for the other ... So our assets are unique and for a visitor who is interested in my assets, I have no doubt that s/he will visit my park in the end. So, you know, cooperating is a win-win solution anyway (Interviewee #5).

5. Relating business cases to cooperation and coopetition: the temporal dimension

The study conducted on tourism destinations significantly contributes to both theoretical discussion and business development of coopetition. In what follows, we illustrate the temporal dimension of coopetition that we could find in our tourism destinations.

Time plays an irreplaceable role in interorganizational dynamics in general and in coopetitive dynamics in particular. It may be exemplified with the following matrix (Figure 1).

Quadrant A is the most interesting quadrant in the matrix as it is a good exemplification of what actually happens in tourism destinations (such as the Santa Claus Village in Rovaniemi) where tourism businesses want to promote the image of a destination as a whole in order to attract tourists to the destination they belong to, while they compete to attract tourists once they have reached the destination.

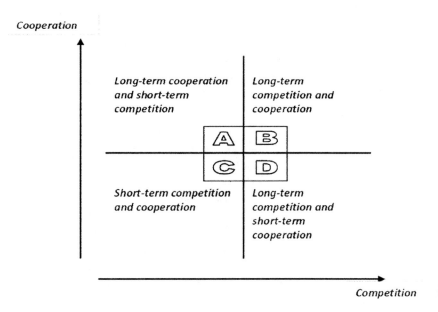

Figure 1. Temporal Dimensions of Coopetition. A includes businesses that compete in the short term and cooperate in the long term (cooperation prevails); B includes businesses that compete and cooperate in the long term (cooperation and competition are balanced in the long term); C includes businesses that compete and cooperate in the short term (cooperation and competition are balanced only in the short term); D includes businesses that compete in the long term and cooperate in the short term (competition prevails).

Our cases illustrate that often long-term cooperation (either imposed by an external actor such a public authority, or achieved voluntarily by individual business) can be beneficial for businesses/firms that are spatially competing and this is even truer for tourism destinations as it enhances the image of the destination itself for end consumers. Nonetheless, cooperation and competition can simultaneously take place and the relative importance of each of the two constituting elements (and their change over time) can influence the very same structure of the sector under consideration, with a strong impact on the nature of interorganizational relationships, the division of labour between organizations, the variety and differentiation of the services and goods provided by the destination as a whole. Last but not least, a tourism destination can continuously re-create itself over time.

The figure provided should not be read in a static way as each quadrant might represent a different stage in the lifecycle of coopetitive strategies. For example, the Italian cases of the theme parks in the Romagna region well illustrate how companies originally included in quadrant D (competing in the long term and cooperating in the short term) later shifted to quadrant B (indeed they started competing and cooperating in the long term). This change produced a positive effect on the destination as a whole, making it more appealing for a number of reasons: (1) the assets on offer are promoted in a more rational and systemic way and (2) the assets on offer are managed through a logic that resembles the one of a portfolio.

For example, the increasing cooperation among theme parks located in the Riviera di Romagna illustrates that by trying to build up its own profile and identity in an attempt to minimize the area of overlapping with its direct competitors, every and each of the theme parks has contributed to differentiate the overall offer of theme park entertainment in the relevant destination. This has contributed to enrich the image of the destination itself.

Interestingly, the temporal angle in coopetition comes into picture when evaluating the seasonal changes and their impact to company behaviour. In the Santa Claus Village, an indicator of (short-term) cooperation has been the fact whether competing companies recommend each other to customers if it happens that they are fully booked, closed, or if they have run out of merchandize. For instance, restaurants have discussed about the opening hours (more complementary hours during low season) and operational logic (another restaurant may host the lunch, while the other may focus more and more on extensive cafeteria offerings) during low season. Hence, temporal dimension can be also analysed from the angle of high season/low season. The entrepreneurs seem to have contrasting views on cooperation and the rationale behind it during different seasons. First, when it is low season you may have to cooperate (e.g. in a marketing campaign or low pricing) to get at least some amount of customers in the region, in the first place. However, more egoistic attitudes can be identified as well, when during low season one wishes to survive by rising upon other's shoulders. Then again, during peak season companies seem to pay less attention to cooperation for everyone's doing quite well anywise, and they are also rather busy. Thus, temporalities of coopetition may evoke intermittent cooperation, even opportunism, among companies.

All in all, in the case of a network product or a territorial destination product experience, competing firms have to evaluate the benefits and possibilities of a cooperative approach. This creates co-existence and simultaneity of competition and cooperation.

6. Conclusion and implications

This study has analysed and captured the logic of temporal dimensions of coopetition. Also, we have tried to identify some key processes (of decision-making and strategic thinking and action) when adopting a coopetitive approach in tourism destinations.

Our analysis provides several significant implications for tourism managers, developers, and policy-makers. Also, our categorizations help the academicians in their theory development. It can be said that in the case of a network product or a territorial destination product, competing firms have to constantly evaluate the benefits and possibilities between a cooperative and competitive approach. Coopetition in tourism destination appears to be a complex process of values, norms, and work practices that is rich in socio-cultural dynamics due to simultaneity (and other temporalities) and co-located nature of tourism production and consumption.

In conclusion, on the basis of our findings we have here gathered some key points that might be useful for tourism destination management and policy-making. Firstly, often cooperation and coopetition among tourism businesses shift from a prevalently short-term basis to a long term one. This often leads to significant benefits to the destination as a whole since synergies sooner or later will be embodied in the perceived unity of the destination. In order for this process to be effective, the local DMOs or entrepreneurial associations should prepare the structural conditions (such as ad hoc incentives and forums for discussion and mutual trust building) useful for enhancing and strengthening collaboration itself.

Secondly, a destination where businesses cooperate or coopete can better showcase the variety of its assets to external stakeholders and can help internal stakeholders to gain awareness of the fact that they are dealing with a portfolio of assets that should be carefully and effectively managed. This may also lead to important status building towards the policy-makers, not only the tourists and tour operators.

The third point deals with institutional conditions that frame coopetition strategies. Our cases show that cooperative ventures in the tourism industry are dependent on both initial processes and external conditions. For instance, as the cases show, the availability of small networks of firms who are clearly willing to cooperate on the basis of mutual trust is vital for the development of cooperation and the destination/network itself. In the case of Mirabilandia (where the management, after the bankruptcy, started looking at other theme parks as coopetitors serving the same destination with entertainment activities and enriching the set of assets offered by the area as a whole), successful coopetition has produced mutual learning. Contrarily, it is not enough if the public sector encourages or even supports cooperation in the destination, if the companies are not committed to the process, as is the case in the Santa Claus Village. This is somewhat surprising, since the companies share a common theme. Altogether, this adds to relevant literature dealing with alliances (Doz, 1996).

Fourthly, we emphasize the role of the public and the semi-public organizations in promotion of coopetitive action in tourism destinations. Indeed, public authorities should work in liaison with the businesses of a certain geographical area in order to help them find the right synergies at the right time. Time is of the essence here as coordination is fundamental in order to supply certain kinds of complex services to the end consumers. The role of the DMO is also central as a coordinating force for cooperation on a local/destination level, and additionally, public funding is often channelled to the region via these organizations.

The fifth point is that managers should be oriented towards long-term cooperation, regardless of any incentive provided by the public authority (e.g. a DMO). Indeed, long-term cooperation is beneficial for businesses because it helps building and strengthening the overall image of the tourism destination and it increases the number of potential visits for the destination itself (this is a variable-sum game, which differs from the short-term constant-sum game which is played between competing businesses, once the number of the visitors of the destination is known). However, cooperation appears to focus on issue/logical reasoning-based rationale over a value/emotional-based one (see Araujo & Brito, 1998; Kylänen & Rusko, 2011; von Friedrichs Grängsjö, 2003). This has a negative impact on long-term bonding of the companies *for* the destination's sake.

Last but not least, our analysis and empirical evidence from the tourism industry show that coopetition formation processes are mostly emergent and unintentional rather than intentional and rationally planned (Kylänen & Rusko, 2011; Mariani, 2007, 2008, 2009). Thus, we support the idea that coopetition can be the by-product of a socio-cultural construction and can display a contingent and complex nature.

The results of the study are still very preliminary and several questions are left on the table, contributing to define a challenging agenda for future research. First, the cases analysed are just a small sample of tourism businesses/destinations. In order to enrich the spectrum of known coopetitive strategies (and related formation processes), we focused on a limited amount of cases in two countries. This can be justified when little is known about a phenomenon (i.e. the temporal dimension of coopetition) and current perspectives seem inadequate since they have little empirical substantiation (Eisenhardt, 1989). Also, our qualitative methodology, in particular long-term ethnography, has supported us in identifying actual activities taken, decisions made and ways of thinking, but also in sketching the overall *coopetitive culture*. Therefore, we have found it valuable to do on-site observation, both participatory and non-participant, in parallel to conducted interviews and available text-based data. The obvious drawback of such a methodological choice is a partial loss of external validity, although in the chosen methodology we are after a credible analysis instead of strict validity. Departing from this premise, it could be interesting to extend our analysis to a larger number of cases in the tourism industry and other industries.

Second, it appears that in encouraging coopetition among firms and organizations that operate in competitive arenas, policy-makers could help to build a stronger brand image for the destination in international markets, but still it is not clear what would be the consequences for domestic markets. This might be a topic for future investigation.

A third interesting topic for future research could be found in moving more in-depth to the logic of complex coopetitive decision-making processes by highlighting the concrete practices that are omnipresent in the locus of territorial strategies and innovation. It seems that temporalities are very much connected to spatial features and elements of tourism destinations. The locus of coopetition comes into the picture as the decisions are not entirely local but also global, involving both near-by (horizontal) and distant (vertical) coopetitors. On the other hand, an in-depth network process analysis could help to illustrate the complexities of coopetitive tourism networks (see, for example, Baggio, 2008).

Finally, it seems to us that strategic learning processes take place in coopetitive contexts where tourism businesses actually learn to cooperate even if before they were purely competing. This theme should deserve much attention in future research: certainly much more than that it has received so far. In the long run, it can also prove to be an important argument for co-located cooperation over fierce competition.

References

Araujo, L., & Brito, C.M. (1998). Agency and constitutional ordering in networks. A case study of the port wine industry. *International Studies of Management and Organisation*, 27(4), 22–46.

Astley, W. (1984). Towards an appreciation of collective strategy. *Academy of Management Review*, 9(3), 526–535.

Astley, W., & Fombrun, C. (1983). Collective strategy: Social ecology of organizational environments. *Academy of Management Review*, 8(4), 576–587.

Baggio, R. (2008). *Network analysis of a tourism destination*. Doctoral Thesis, University of Queensland.

Barnett, W.P., Mischke, G.A., & Ocasio, W. (2000). The evolution of collective strategies among organizations. *Organization Studies*, 21(2), 325–354.

Becattini, G. (2002). Industrial sectors and industrial districts: Tools for industrial analysis. *European Planning Studies*, 10(4), 483–493.

Bengtsson, M., & Kock, S. (2000). Coopetition in business networks – to cooperate and compete simultaneously. *Industrial Marketing Management*, 29(5), 411–425.

Brandenburger, A.M., & Nalebuff, B.J. (1996). *Co-opetition*. New York: Doubleday.

Brandenburger, A.M., & Stuart, S. (1996). Value-based business strategy. *Journal of Economical Management Strategy*, 5(1), 5–14.

Bresser, R. (1988). Matching collective and competitive strategies. *Strategic Management Journal*, 9, 375–385.

Contractor, F.J. & Lorange, P. (1988). Why should firms cooperate? The strategy and economic basis for cooperative ventures. In F.J. Contractor and P. Lorange, editors, *Cooperative Strategies in International Business*. Chicago, IL: Lexington, MA: Lexington Books: 3–30.

Dacin, T., Oliver, C., & Roy, J.-P. (2007). The legitimacy of strategic alliances: an institutional perspective. *Strategic Management Journal*, 28, 169–187.

Dagnino, G.B., & Rocco, E. (Eds.). (2009). *Coopetition strategy. Theory, experiments and cases*. London: Routledge.

Doz, Y.L. (1996). The evolution of cooperation in strategic alliances: Initial conditions, or learning processes? *Strategic Management Journal*, 17, 55–83.

Eisenhardt, K.M. (1989). Building theory from case study research. *Academy of Management Review*, 14, 532–550.

Eriksson, P., & Kovalainen, A. (2008). *Qualitative methods in business research*. London: Sage.

Fyall, A., & Garrod, B. (2005). *Tourism marketing. A collaborative approach*. Aspects of Tourism 18 Clevedon: Channel View Publications.

Garcia-Canal, E., Duarte, C.L., Criado, J.R., & Llaneza, A.V. (2002). Accelerating international expansion through global alliances: A typology of cooperative strategies. *Journal of World Business*, 37, 91–107.

García-Rosell, J.-C., Haanpää, M., Kylänen, M., & Markuksela, V. (2007). From firms to extended markets – A cultural approach to tourism product development. *Tourism*, 55(4), 445–459.

Glaser, B.G., & Strauss, L. (1967). *The discovery of grounded theory*. Chicago, IL: Aldine Publishing.

Gnyawali, D.R., & Madhavan, R. (2001). Cooperative networks and competitive dynamics: A structural embeddedness perspective. *Academy of Management Review*, 26(3), 431–445.

Hakansson, H., & Snehota, I. (1995). *Developing relationships in business networks*. London: Routledge.

Hammersley, M., & Atkinson, P. (1995). *Ethnography. Principles in practice*. London: Routledge.

Higgins-Desbiolles, F. (2006). More than an industry: Tourism as a social force. *Tourism Management*, 27(6), 1192–1208.

Hjalager, A.-M. (2000). Tourism destinations and the concept of industrial districts. *Tourism and Hospitality Research*, 2(3), 199–213.

Kylänen, M. (2007). Enlightening Christmas experience – reflections on the experience pyramid. In M. Kylänen (Ed.), *Articles on experiences 3. Christmas experiences* (pp. 100–122). Rovaniemi: Lapland Centre of Expertise for the Experience Industry.

Kylänen, M., & Rusko, R. (2011). Unintentional and concealed coopetition. The case of Pyhä-Luosto tourism destination in the Finnish Lapland. *European Management Journal*, 29, 193–205.

Lado, A., Boyd, N., & Hanlon, S. (1997). Competition, cooperation, and the search for economic rents: A syncretic model. *Academy of Management Review*, 22(1), 110–141.

Lavie, D. (2006). The competitive advantage of interconnected firms: An extension of the resource-based view. *Academy of Management Review*, *31*(3), 638–658.

LEO Finland (2010). Branding a place – from words to actions. A Finnish report on development of Rovaniemi Christmas brand. Tourism and Experience Management Cluster. Rovaniemi: National Centre of Expertise Programme. http://www.experiencebusiness.fi

Luo, Y. (2005). Towards coopetition within a multinational enterprise: A perspective from foreign subsidiaries. *Journal of World Business*, *40*(1), 71–90.

Mariani, M.M. (2007). Coopetition as an emergent strategy: Empirical evidence from a consortium of Italian opera houses. *International Studies of Management and Organization*, *37*(2), 97–126.

Mariani, M.M. (2008). Induced coopetition and emergent cooperation: An international study on the opera houses sector. *Public*, *15*, May, 1–7.

Mariani, M.M. (2009). Emergent coopetitive and cooperative strategies in inter-organizational relationships: Empirical evidence from Australian and Italian operas. In G.B. Dagnino & E. Rocco (Eds.), *Coopetition strategy. Theory, experiments and cases* (pp. 166–190). London: Routledge.

Miles, M., & Huberman, A.M. (1984). *Qualitative data analysis*. Beverly Hills, CA: Sage.

Nason, J., & Golding, D. (1998). Approaching observation. In G. Symon & C. Cassell (Eds.), *Qualitative methods and analysis in organizational research. A practical guide* (pp. 234–249). London: Sage.

Pettigrew, A.M. (1990). Longitudinal field research on change: Theory and practice. *Organization Science*, *1*(3), 267–292.

Powell, W.W., Koput, K.W., & Smith-Doerr, L. (1996). Inter-organizational collaboration and the locus of innovation: Networks of learning in biotechnology. *Administrative Science Quarterly*, *41*, 116–145.

Pretes, M. (1995). Postmodern tourism: The Santa Claus industry. *Annals of Tourism Research*, *22*(1), 1–15.

Pretes, M. (2007). Santa Claus tourism in Lapland. In M. Kylänen (Ed.), *Articles on experiences 3. Christmas experiences* (pp. 22–31). Rovaniemi: Lapland Centre of Expertise for the Experience Industry.

Reur, J.J., & Ariño, A. (2007). Strategic alliance contracts: Dimensions and determinants of contractual complexity. *Strategic Management Journal*, *28*(3), 313–330.

Staber, U. (1998). Inter-firm co-operation and competition in industrial districts. *Organization Studies*, *19*(4), 701–724.

Stamboulis, Y., & Skayannis, P. (2003). Innovation strategies and technology for experience-based tourism. *Tourism Management*, *24*(1), 35–43.

Strauss, A. (1987). *Qualitative analysis for social scientists*. Cambridge: Cambridge University Press.

Van Laere, K., & Heene, A. (2003). Social networks as a source of competitive advantage for the firm. *Journal of Management Learning*, *15*(6), 248–258.

van Maanen, J. (1979). The fact of fiction in organisational ethnography. *Administrative Science Quarterly*, *24*, 539–550.

von Friedrichs Grängsjö, Y. (2003). Destination networking: Co-opetition in peripheral surroundings. *International Journal of Physical Distribution and Logistics Management*, *33*(5), 427–448.

von Friedrichs Grängsjö (2001). Destinationsmarknadsföring: En studie av turism ur ett producentperspektiv, *Dissertation* No 7. Stockholms Universitet: (Edsbruk: Akademi litteratur).

Wang, Y. (2008). Collaborative destination marketing: Understanding the dynamic process. *Journal of Travel Research*, *47*(2), 151–166.

Wang, Y., & Krakover, S. (2007). Destination marketing: Competition, cooperation or coopetition? *International Journal of Contemporary Hospitality Management*, *20*(2), 126–141.

Zaheer, S. (1995). Overcoming the liability of foreignness. *Academy of Management Journal*, *38*, 341–363.

Ranking assessment systems for responsible tourism products and corporate social responsibility practices

Mara Manente, Valeria Minghetti and Erica Mingotto

CISET – Ca' Foscari University, Villa Mocenigo, Riviera San Pietro 83, 30030 Oriago di Mira (VE), Italy

Responsible tourism and corporate social responsibility (CSR) have a significant role in promoting the integration of sustainable practices in the tourism industry. The paper presents the results of a study carried out on reporting programmes assessing the "responsibility level" of tourism companies. It aims at developing a tool to encourage and support enterprises, especially small companies, in behaving in a more responsible way and adopt systems to assess their business responsibility. After an overview of the literature regarding the concept of responsible tourism and CSR and a description of the reporting programmes, a quantitative model (the analytic hierarchy process) has been implemented to clarify the main attributes, the strengths, and the weaknesses of the assessment systems and to determine their overall effectiveness with respect to different criteria.

1. Introduction

Promoting development, with respect to the environment and cultural heritage while supporting the well-being and growth of local communities, is a crucial issue for the evolution of modern tourism. This inevitably implies responsible behaviour both by tourists and by businesses involved in travel production and distribution. Responsible tourism and corporate social responsibility (CSR) can, as a consequence, play a significant role for the sustainable development of tourism. The international community and institutions such as the European Union (EU) are therefore inviting the tourism industry to implement CSR as part of their business strategy and to offer responsible tourism products.

The development of responsible tourism and the spread of CSR in the tourism industry have produced the need to build specific tools to assess and certify the economic, social, and environmental performances of tourism companies. Despite the role that assessment programmes play, few tourism enterprises have so far opted to adopt them, small and medium enterprises (SMEs) in particular. Furthermore, many of these assessment systems use different and varied approaches and are not based on agreed international standards (Dodds & Joppe, 2005). Nevertheless, according to the literature, their importance in stimulating the tourism industry to follow a responsible development path is unquestionable (Goodwin, 2005; Kalish, 2002).

But what are the attributes that characterize these reporting systems and what are the most effective programmes? And are these assessment systems suitable for SMEs or are they too expensive and complex to implement? A research study, carried out by CISET (International Centre for Studies on Tourism Economics) within the EU Grant Programme European Alliance for Responsible Tourism and Hospitality, has tried to answer these questions and some of the results are presented in this paper. The study is intended to be a tool of support for tourism operators, especially for small businesses, to help them identify the best programmes that respond to their specific business characteristics and mission.

The aim of the paper is to propose and explain the method that we have adopted to identify the main characteristics of the schemes and to measure their effectiveness in evaluating the "responsibility level" of tourism companies, while also considering if these tools can be easily implemented by SMEs. The paper is divided into three parts. The first one clarifies the concepts of responsible tourism and CSR, since many definitions have been formulated, creating confusion and misunderstanding. The second part explains the context of existing assessment systems and the main aspects. Finally, the third part describes the analytic hierarchy process (AHP) model and the results of its application.

2. Responsible tourism and CSR

Despite the fact that tourism represents a very important industry, which contributes to global GDP (Gross Domestic Product) and creates jobs, it also produces negative and serious impacts at economic, social, and environmental levels, due to uncontrolled development (Akama & Kieti, 2007; Kasim, 2006), which generates a volume of flows higher than the destination carrying capacity (Costa, Manente, & Furlan, 2001). As a consequence, at the beginning of the 1980s, at the same time as the spread of sustainable tourism, the concept of responsible tourism started to emerge (Anderek et al., 2007; Del Chiappa, Grappi, & Romani, 2009). According to Budeanu, it represents a reaction to negative effects produced by mass tourism, a new way to conceive holidays (as cited in Del Chiappa et al., 2009), driving a growing number of people to make choices, and to behave according to values such as consciousness, sobriety, and respect (Franch, Sambri, Martini, Pegan, & Rizzi, 2008).

Different definitions of responsible tourism have been given over time (Del Chiappa, Grappi & Romani, 2009; Kasim, 2006) and numerous concepts of other similar forms of tourism have proliferated (Responsible Travel Handbook, 2006), making the understanding of what responsible tourism is more complicated. According to the Cape Town Declaration (2002), later reviewed by the Kerala Declaration in 2008, responsible tourism takes a variety of forms, but it always refers to travel and tourism that minimize negative environmental, social, and cultural impacts; that generate greater economic benefits for local people by improving working conditions and access to the industry; that involve local people in decisions that affect their lives and life chances; that make positive contributions to the conservation of natural and cultural heritage and to the maintenance of the world's diversity; that provide more enjoyable experiences for tourists through more meaningful connections with local people and a greater understanding of local cultural and environmental issues; that provide access for physically challenged people; and that are culturally sensitive and engender respect between tourists and hosts.

The definition given by the International Coalition for Responsible Tourism is similar: responsible tourism is a form of tourism, which respects and preserves in the long-term, natural, cultural, and social resources and which contributes in a positive and fair way to the development and welfare of those people who live, work, and spend their holidays in a particular destination (http://www.coalition-tourisme-responsable.org/tourisme-respons able.html).

The principles of responsible tourism are also shared by other alternative forms of tourism, such as ecotourism, community-based tourism, fair tourism and rural tourism, even though every form emphasizes one aspect rather another one. For example, ecotourism focuses on environmental preservation, but it does not forget the value of respect, fairness, and equity towards the local community. Fair tourism believes that benefits from tourism have to be shared more equitably between the tourism industry and the host community in the destination, but it does not ignore the other values of responsible tourism (see the Responsible Travel Handbook, 2006). As a consequence, it could be stated that all these alternative forms of tourism can be considered as a responsible way of travelling and included in a broad definition of responsible tourism. The basic elements are the same, but every form of tourism gives them a different importance.

The concept of CSR has developed since the mid-1990s outside the tourism industry, as an essential framework for changing management practice in general. According to experts, CSR can help companies both to increase their competitive advantage and to contribute to sustainable development (Kalish, 2002). Several definitions of CSR have been proposed over the years. The World Business Council for Sustainable Development, for instance, acknowledges that CSR is "the continuing commitment by business to behave ethically and contribute to economic development while improving the quality of life of the workforce and of their families as well as of the local community and society at large" (WBCSD, 1999).

The European Commission, recognizing the role of CSR as a contributing factor to the Lisbon Strategy for growth and jobs, asserts that CSR is "a concept whereby companies integrate social and environmental concerns in their business operations and in their interaction with their stakeholders on a voluntary basis" (EC COM, 2001, 366, p. 6). CSR is about integrating social, economic, and environmental concerns at the same time into the enterprise's activities; it should not be separate from business strategy and operations; it is a voluntary concept and it is about the interaction between the company and its internal and external stakeholders (EC COM, 2001, 366, p. 6).

The definitions underline that beyond maximizing profits, businesses have to act with regard to employees, the local community, the environment and other stakeholders. As a consequence, while in the past the "financial bottom line" was the only one acknowledged, now it is common to use the term "triple bottom line": companies have to be aware of the economic, social, and environmental impacts they produce with their activities (Kalish, 2002). The definitions also show that CSR has to be integrated in every aspect of the business, from strategy to human resources policy, from selection of suppliers to relation- ships with consumers, competitors, and the community.

Although CSR and responsible tourism originate from different contexts and motives, they share the same principles. For a company, both proposing travel and tourism services coherent with the values of responsible tourism and integrating CSR in its business, means behaving in a respectful, ethical, and fair way towards its stakeholders and the environment. For this reason, we have considered reporting programmes that refer both with respect to responsible tourism and to the implementation of CSR.

In spite of the fact that the EU and the United Nations Foundation consider CSR strategic for the sustainability and competitiveness of the travel and tourism industry (Ermlich, 2009), CSR standards and practices are not widely implemented and widespread in the tourism industry (Dodds & Joppe, 2005; Kalish, 2002). While international hotel companies and large tour operators have already adopted CSR, SMEs find it difficult to organize their core business in a socially and ecologically responsible way and to develop the conditions under which their activity can be defined as "responsible" (Ermlich, 2009). They often do not have appropriate knowledge and skills or a sufficient budget to invest in long-term planning, as a CSR strategy requires, or to support the certification costs (Dodds & Joppe, 2005). As a consequence, we have not forgotten this problem in evaluating the effectiveness of the reporting systems.

3.   Assessment systems for tourism company responsibility

A reporting system can be defined as a tool that checks and assures that an activity or a product is of specific standards (Bien, 2008). There are many schemes regarding tourism that relate to sustainability (Green Globe, Blue Flag, etc.), and a number of other projects are in the pilot or development phase in different parts of the world. Many of these systems only focus on the environmental dimension (eco-certifications) or on the social dimension. In this paper, we pay attention only to those programmes that refer to the overall responsibility of a company, including all the three dimensions: social, economic, and environmental.

Although assessment programmes share some similar components, they can differ considerably. In particular, we can make two distinctions. The first is represented by the evaluation system (first-party audit vs. second-party and third-party audits); the first-party audit is a self-evaluation carried out by the company; the second-party audit implies that clients (through a customer satisfaction analysis) and/or the industry body ensure that the company (or its product) meets specific standards; the third-party audit means instead that the evaluation is conducted by a neutral and independent certification body. As a consequence, this last type assures greater transparency, objectivity, and credibility (Bien, 2008).

The second element of differentiation is the object of the certification programme (product-based vs. process-based system or process-based vs. performance-based system); product standards reflect the appropriate attributes a product is expected to have, while process standards refer to the appropriate characteristics of the process put in place, from the creation of the goods to the final distribution. Process standards certify businesses that have established and documented systems for ensuring improvement in their performance, but they do not determine any specific performance results. Consequently, businesses receive a certification for their efforts, not for their actual results. Performance-based systems instead certify whether or not a company or an activity complies with objectives outside criteria. On the one hand, performance-based systems are generally less expensive and more suitable for SMEs and allow comparisons to be made between businesses, because they are based on common and objective criteria. On the other hand, process standards stimulate companies to reflect on the more effective and efficient policies for improving their performance (Bien, 2008).

On the basis of this last element of differentiation, reporting methodologies for responsible tourism or CSR in tourism companies can also differ for another important aspect, i.e. the approach they adopt: we can actually distinguish the "certification approach" from the "responsible tourism approach" (Goodwin, 2005). Systems based on the certification approach are generally process oriented, and are more useful for companies that want to audit their internal processes and supply chain and to improve their management strategies. They rarely give holidaymakers, who often do not see the difference year on year, an enhanced experience (Goodwin, 2005). By contrast, programmes based on a responsible tourism approach adopt a market-driven perspective, reflecting the appropriate characteristics a responsible tourism product is expected to have. This latter approach responds better to tourists who demand a more authentic encounter with the environment and the community, based on values of respect for other people and their places (Goodwin, 2005).

While the first approach does not produce significant differentiation in products and does not bring considerable marketing advantages, the second approach is able to really distinguish responsible tourism travel products and the companies that produce them (Goodwin, 2005). The responsible tourism approach and the certification approach are not incompatible or mutually exclusive and some tourism operators have tried to combine them. This distinction is important because other elements and aspects of an assessment system depend on the approach: from priorities on the environmental, social, and economic dimensions to the indicators chosen, from the type of audit to the companies the programme is addressed to.

3.1. *Overview of the main assessment systems for responsible tourism and CSR*

Starting from the review of literature, the study focuses on the assessment systems that evaluate (and eventually certify) the overall responsibility of tourism companies, in particular tour operators, in terms of respect for responsible tourism principles and/or implementation of CSR. The reporting systems analysed have been developed (or are in the elaboration phase) by important European organizations who promote sustainable development and the spread of responsible practices in the tourism industry.

Some of these programmes have been devised by associations of tour operators specialized in responsible tourism or who are engaged in adopting more responsible activities. In this first group, there are the "Responsible Tourism Standards" of the Italian Association for Responsible Tourism (AITR-Associazzione Italiana Turismo Responsible); the methodology of the French Association for Fair and Solidarity Tourism (ATES-Association pour le tourism equitable et solidaire); the "ATR Certification Program" of the French Association of Thematic Tour Operators (ATT-Association des Tour Opérateurs Thématiques); the "Tour Operators' Sector Supplement" developed by the Tour Operator Initiative (TOI), in cooperation with the Global Reporting Initiative (GRI); the system of the English Association of Independent Tour Operators (AITO); and the "Travelife Project", supported by the UK Federation of Tour Operators (FTO).

The other systems have been developed by consulting companies or organizations that propose tools to promote responsibility in tourism businesses. In this second group, there are the "Enterprise Indicator for Responsible Tourism" of the Spanish consulting company QUIDAMTUR; the "CSR Reporting Standards in Tourism" of the German Centre for Environment and Development (KATE-Kontaktstelle fur Umwelt und Entwiklung); and the Responsibletravel.com evaluation programme, the first online travel agency specialized in responsible tourism. Even though these nine systems do not cover all the existing programmes, they are the most representative and they allow us to describe the different contexts and to highlight a significant variety. The main attributes of the reporting tools are described in Tables 1 and 2, where aims, evaluation object, type of audit, and number of indicators are underlined.

The study and the comparison of the systems have shown that there are five main elements of differentiation. The first is represented by the approach used. Figure 1 shows that while the programmes of KATE (Fuchs et al., 2008), TOI-GRI (GRI, 2002), and Travelife are completely based on the certification approach, the only one that follows a totally responsible tourism perspective is the system of AITR, which assesses the package tour. The other methodologies are the result of the integration of the two approaches, and at a different level they try to combine a market-driven perspective with greater attention to the processes and activities developed by the tour operator.

The second element of differentiation is represented by the type of tour operators the programmes are addressed to. The study has actually shown that the systems of AITR, ATES,

Table 1. General comparison of the reporting programmes.

	AITR	ATES	QUIDAMTUR	KATE	ATT
Main objectives	• Distinguish r.t. (Responsible Tourism) from other forms of tourism • Protect consumers, ensuring that the travels respect principles of r.t. • Protect AITR members from other TOs' (Tour Operators) use of r.t. only for marketing reasons • Provide AITR members with a set of minimal operational standards	• Share a common vision among members • Promote transparency, informing travellers that ATES members respect r.t. • Enhance the credibility of ATES members with public opinion	• Assess the level of responsibility of TOs and of tourist enterprises along the tourism value chain • Develop an unambiguous tool, universally applicable, to evaluate the sustainability of tourist services developed	• Spread the principles of sustainability and CSR in tourism • Help TOs to build an integrated responsible strategy to assess and monitor their performance • Give transparency on ecological, social, and economic impacts of business • Ensure comparability and verifiability • Increase credibility among customers • Set up a acknowledged certification system	• Support the development of sustainable and quality tourism • Monitor the economic impacts • Respect heritage, environment and culture • Develop public awareness transparently
Evaluation object	The travel package	The TO structure and the project carried out	Each tourist unit along the package supply chain	The TO CSR	The TO structure and organization
Axes/principles	5	3	4	–	4
Criteria	13	10	54	8	16
Indicators	23	29	98	57	24
Assessment system	Self-evaluation and approval by AITR	Self-evaluation and approval by ATES	Self-evaluation, assessment by clients, and assessment by local TAs (Travel Agencies)	Third-part audit	Third-part audit

Table 2. General comparison of the reporting programmes.

	TOI	Responsibletravel	AITO	Travelife
Main objectives	• Integrate sustainable development into TO business practice • Create a reliable reporting system, which can be used by enterprises of all sizes and nationality	• Product and distribute responsible travels, which create new income and job opportunities for local communities and minimize negative impacts • Select and control partners	• Increase the engagement of their members towards r.t.	• Help TOs and their suppliers to operate according to the principles of r.t. • Inform customers
Evaluation object	The TO CSR	The TO, its policies, and the characteristics of its travels	The TO: its policies and practices of r.t.	The TO, its social, and environmental performance and its suppliers
Axes/principles	–	–	–	8
Criteria	5	4	5	17
Indicators	126	14	Not available	139
Assessment system	Self-evaluation	Self-evaluation and approval by Responsibletravel.com	Self-evaluation and approval by AITO	Self-evaluation and approval by Travelife

and ATT aim at assessing and eventually certifying only tour operators specialized in responsible tourism, while the others have been created for any tour operator wishing to monitor its responsibility. The third element is the priority given to every dimension of responsibility (social, environmental, and economic). The programmes which give more importance to the social aspect are those of AITR, ATES, and ATT: they, in particular, use a set of specific indicators to assess interaction between the company and the local community and cultural exchange between tourists and local people. We can state that this element depends on the fact that the members of these associations are specialized in responsible tourism, for which these aspects are strategic. The programme of Travelife focuses instead on the environmental dimension such as those of KATE and QUIDAMTUR (Villagrán et al., 2010), which also cover the economic aspect better than the others. In contrast with the others, the TOI-GRI assessment scheme develops all three dimensions of responsibility with a sufficient set of indicators.

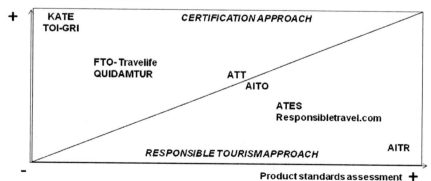

Figure 1. Certification approach versus responsible tourism approach.

The fourth element of differentiation is represented by the type of audit. The only schemes which imply an assessment carried out by a third, independent, and neutral party are those of KATE and ATT. As a consequence, these programmes are more transparent than the other systems, for which the self-evaluation or the second-part audit is sufficient. The last aspect which distinguishes the systems is the degree of implementation of the procedure by SMEs. This element is very important, since small businesses represent about 90% of European tourism industry enterprises and the fact that they meet a lot of difficulty in implementing responsible practices (Dodds & Joppe, 2005; Miller, 2001). Among all the programmes considered in the study, reporting systems such as those of TOI-GRI, Travelife, and KATE could not easily be applied by small tour operators; they are complex and costly in terms of time, and human and financial resources are needed to apply the system and collect the necessary information for developing the numerous set of indicators required.

It is evident that there is a plethora of different programmes and schemes that can be adopted by tourism businesses to assess and address their commitment to responsible tourism and CSR towards clients and stakeholders. Although a large number of local schemes is desirable because it represents the cultural and ecological diversity of countries (Goodwin, 2005), so much variety can be perplexing and meet resistance on the part of tour organizations and tourists (Dodds & Joppe, 2005).

4. Methodology

The study and the comparison of the assessment systems for responsible tourism and CSR have clarified the main attributes that characterize the schemes. It is difficult with a qualitative analysis to determine an overall judgement that clarifies whether every reporting programme is effective and appropriate for monitoring the "responsibility level" of tourism businesses. This difficulty depends on the presence of different criteria, by which the validity of the programmes should be evaluated, and on the fact that all the systems function well with regard to some parameters, but are deficient with regard to other aspects. As a consequence, a quantitative model can help in better understanding the strengths and weaknesses of the reporting systems and in defining a value that represents their overall effectiveness. The final results could give some clear guidelines to those who are looking for more detailed information about the assessment systems. Tour operators, particularly small businesses, can benefit from this support in the selection process to help in deciding which programmes are the most appropriate for their needs.

4.1 The model

Given that the assessment systems in question are characterized and distinguished by many different aspects and that it is the integration of these aspects that confers effectiveness and validity, it follows that it is necessary to evaluate the reporting programmes in relation to several variables. We need a model capable of evaluating assessment frameworks on the basis of multi-decision criteria to which different levels of importance can be attributed. From among all the models currently available, the model chosen to evaluate and rank the reporting programmes is AHP, developed by Thomas Saaty in the 1970s. It is part of the family of multi-criteria models and it can be defined as a methodology that evaluates the overall performance of different alternatives (in this case, the assessment systems), by giving a final score to each individual alternative, obtained by adding together the sum of points achieved with respect to each set of criteria (Saaty, 1990a; Saaty, 1990b).

The AHP model is a valid support to decision makers, because it allows them to successfully manage the complexity of the decisional process and to arrive at the most suitable choice. This explains the reasons behind the decision to adopt the AHP model. The purpose of the proposed tool is not just to supply a ranking of systems; it should also be seen as a guide for operators who wish to compare the different assessment systems at their disposal and to decide which one would be the best to use. The AHP model is based on a six-step procedure: first, identifying the goal to be achieved; second, defining criteria and any eventual sub-criteria considered to be important for the choice; third, identifying possible alternative decisions; fourth, determining how much weight to give the alternatives in relation to the established criteria; fifth, determining the weight of the decision criteria in relation to the goal; and sixth, constructing the ranking from the possible alternatives.

4.1.1. Defining goal, criteria, and alternatives

The first three phases lead towards the construction of a dominance hierarchy. This involves a reticular structure composed of several levels, where the first (the one at the top) represents the goal of the assessment, while the second contains the criteria by which the alternatives are evaluated. Each of these can, in turn, be subdivided into more specific sub-criteria and so on, until arriving at the base of the structure where, directly linked to more specific parameters, we find all the different alternatives.

The choice of criteria represents a crucial phase in the construction of the entire model, given that opting for certain parameters rather than others will create significant differences in the final ranking. For the evaluation of the reporting systems of CSR and responsible tourism, four main criteria are proposed and, according with the preliminary study, they are considered the most important variables for the efficacy of an assessment system (Table 3).

The first criterion is the degree of coverage given to the three elements of responsible business: given the fact that business responsibility depends on three dimensions, social, economic, and environmental, the assessment programmes must be capable of assessing all these aspects with appropriate indicators. This criterion is divided into other three sub-criteria, which in turn is divided into further sub-criteria.

The second parameter is the degree of implementation of responsible business practices on the part of SMEs: given the difficulty that SMEs meet in implementing responsible practices, the assessment systems must also be evaluated in relation to their applicability for SMEs. This second criterion is also composed of two sub-criteria. The third criterion is the level of integration between the certification approach and that of responsible tourism: the integration of the two approaches allows us to gather together simultaneously all the aspects of responsibility and to disseminate pertinent information to all the stakeholders, from tourists to the host community, and from suppliers to employees. The fourth parameter is the type of auditing: the fourth and final decision criterion is the type of assessment that tour operators will be subjected to by the programmes, given that the type of auditing determines the reliability and transparency of the certification programme.

The alternatives are represented by the reporting systems considered in the study: (A) the programme of AITR, (B) the programme of ATES, (C) the programme of QUIDAMTUR, (D) the programme of KATE, (E) the programme of ATT, (F) the programme of GRI, (G) the programme of Responsibletravel.com, and (H) the programme of Travelife.

4.1.2. Defining the priorities of alternatives

Step 4 consists in establishing the priorities of the alternatives, in other words, in assigning to them a numerical value that expresses their suitability compared to the other options

Table 3.   Set of criteria and sub-criteria.

Criterion 1: Degree of coverage given to the three elements of responsible business
1.1. The environmental element: the presence of one or more indicators as listed below
1.1.1. Indicators to verify whether the company has an environmental policy in place
1.1.2. Indicators to check the measures adopted by the company with regard to its supply chain and the environment
1.1.3. Indicators inherent to energy consumption, water, paper, and the recycling of water, paper, and other materials carried out by the company
1.1.4. Indicators with regard to CO_2 emissions produced by the company and the measures adopted by the company to reduce or compensate for the emissions by financing projects to safeguard the environment
1.1.5. Indicators regarding information given out by the company to employees, suppliers, the local community, and tourists concerning environmental-friendly behaviour and any environmental problems in holiday destinations
1.1.6. Indicators in relation to the measures adopted by the company to prevent/reduce negative impacts on the environment as a result of tourist activities in holiday destinations
1.2. The social element: the presence of one or more of the indicators as listed below
1.2.1. Indicators in relation to the measures adopted by the company to ensure healthy and safe working conditions for employees as well as offering opportunities for training courses
1.2.2. Indicators with regard to personnel (e.g. the percentage of women in managerial positions, turnover rates, the percentage of job-related accidents and incidents of illness, rate of staff satisfaction)
1.2.3. Indicators in relation to the measures adopted by the company to control whether suppliers have strategies in place to guarantee the safety and well-being of their employees
1.2.4. Indicators aimed at establishing whether the company maintains fair and lasting business relations with their suppliers
1.2.5. Indicators aimed at verifying whether the company acts in the interests of the local community by evaluating existing social problems in the destination and encouraging the local community to be proactively involved in the organization of holidays in the destination
1.2.6. Indicators in relation to the measures adopted by the company to inform tourists about the social and cultural aspects of the destination and whether any meetings or occasions for cultural exchange between tourists and local people are planned and integrated into the holiday package
1.2.7. Indicators regarding measures adopted to ensure clients' safety and satisfaction
1.3. The economic element: the presence of one or more of the indicators as listed below
1.3.1. Quantitative indicators with regard to business performance (e.g. total revenue, percentage of income derived from responsible tourism (if offered), sales of package holidays, main source of income, overheads/expenditure, number of employees, etc.)
1.3.2. Indicators that demonstrate the economic contribution made by the company to the holiday destination in terms of funding development projects and programmes, hiring local people, buying local products, and the relationships established with local suppliers
Criterion 2: Degree of implementation of responsible business practices on the part of SMEs
2.1. Cost of adhering to and implementing the report
2.2. Simplicity
2.2.1. The number of indicators used by the programme
2.2.2. The ease of data collection and construction of indicators
Criterion 3: Level of integration between certification approach and responsible tourism one
Criterion 4: Type of auditing (carried out by an independent third party; ratified by a business partner or self-assessment by the company itself)

---

for each of the evaluation criteria. For example, the priorities calculated with respect to the second criterion show whether the reporting programmes considered can be easily adopted by SMEs; the higher the value (at most equal to 1), the more suitable are the programmes. The AHP model traces the priorities of each of the options making pair-wise comparisons, in other words, comparing two by two all the alternatives, with respect to each single sub-criterion and questioning whether one is preferable to another and to what extent. The operation must be entrusted to experts familiar with the subject, who will be asked to express their preferences according to a scale developed by Saaty:

1 if alternative i and alternative j are equal;
3 if alternative i is moderately preferable to alternative j;
5 if alternative i is strongly preferable to alternative j;
7 if alternative i is more strongly preferable to alternative j;
9 if alternative i is extremely preferable to alternative j;
2, 4, 6, 8 as intermediate values (or in the case of compromise).

The result of the comparison is the coefficient of dominance a_{ij}, an estimate of the dominance of the alternative i compared to j. In particular, making a paired comparison of n elements results in n^2 coefficients, of which only $n(n-1)/2$ must be directly determined by the expert who is carrying out the evaluation, in that

$$a_{ii} = 1 \text{ and } a_{ji} = 1/a_{ij} \text{ for each of the values of } i \text{ and } j.$$

The coefficients of dominance determine therefore a positive reciprocal square matrix, **A**, with n rows and n columns (where n is equal to the number of alternatives) called "matrix of paired comparisons". At this point, it is necessary to standardize the matrix of paired comparisons, calculating the sum of each of the columns and dividing each element of the matrix by the value of the sum of the vector column to which that particular element belongs. Finally, we can calculate the average of each row of the standardized matrix, obtaining in this way the vector of weights, **w**.

Before relying completely on the calculated weights, Saaty requires the consistency of the original matrix to be verified, i.e. that the assigning of preferences has been coherent throughout the comparison. It is therefore essential to verify that the degree of inconsistency is not too high and in order to do this, it is necessary firstly to multiply the matrix of the paired comparisons A (not standardized) by the vector of weights, **w**, in order to obtain the vector **Aw**; secondly to divide the vector **Aw** by the vector of the weights **w**, to obtain the vector $\boldsymbol{\lambda}_{max}$; finally to find the average of the values that make up vector $\boldsymbol{\lambda}_{max}$ in order to obtain an average $\boldsymbol{\lambda}_{max}$.

When the matrix is perfectly consistent, $\boldsymbol{\lambda}_{max} = n$, i.e. to the number of elements that must be compared. When this does not happen, it is necessary to calculate the two indices specifically developed by Saaty, the consistency index (CI) and the consistency ratio (CR). If CR ≤ 0.10, the degree of inconsistency in the paired comparisons matrix is acceptable, and it is therefore possible to assume that the priorities obtained are significant. If on the other hand, CR > 0.10, it may be that serious inconsistencies exist in the paired comparisons, and as a consequence, the analysis may not bring relevant results:

$$CI = \frac{(\boldsymbol{\lambda}_{max} - n)}{(n-1)}, \quad CR = \frac{CI}{RI}.$$

RI is the random index, a predetermined value that depends on the number of alternatives.

Following the described procedure, we have obtained the priorities of each of the alternatives with respect to the sub-criteria of parameters 1 and 2 and to criteria 3 and 4. All the matrices present a CR < 0.10 and in some cases also equal to zero; as a consequence, the priorities can be considered to be consistent and acceptable.

4.1.3. Defining the weight of decision criteria

Establishing the weight of the criteria means assigning to them a numerical value that illustrates their importance with respect to the established goal. The procedure is the same described as for Step 4. In our analysis, we have decided that the sub-criteria have the same importance, and as a consequence the same priorities, with respect to the criterion on which they depend. The main four criteria instead have different relevance; in our opinion parameter 1 should be considered the most important one, given that an effective reporting scheme should have a sufficient set of indicators for each of the three dimensions in order to check the overall responsibility of the company. The weights, calculated from the pairwise comparisons, are shown in Table 4.

4.1.4. Determining the final ranking

Finally in Step 6, in order to determine the overall priority of each of the reporting systems in relation to the initial goal and to draw up a final ranking, it is necessary to multiply the local weights of each element with those of the superior elements, and then to add the results. After obtaining the priorities of each of the alternatives with respect to the four main criteria (Table 5), it is possible to calculate the final ranking, multiplying the priorities with the weights of parameters.

5. Results

According to the calculated weights, the alternative E, i.e. the programme of ATT is the best alternative because it reaches the highest priority (0.139, the bold value in Table 5); in other words, it satisfies the main decision criteria better than the other options. This does not mean that ATT is perfect in every criteria, but that it is able to combine these aspects better than the other alternatives. The second and the third positions are, respectively,

Table 4.   Weights of the four main criteria.

	W
1	0.53
2	0.30
3	0.11
4	0.06

Table 5.   Priorities of alternatives with respect to the four main criteria and final ranking.

	Partial priorities				
	P1	P2	P3	P4	Final ranking
A	0.10	0.22	0.02	0.06	0.123
B	0.11	0.20	0.13	0.06	0.135
C	0.15	0.05	0.20	0.13	0.122
D	0.16	0.05	0.02	0.31	0.120
E	0.09	0.11	0.33	0.31	**0.139**
F	0.22	0.02	0.02	0.02	0.127
G	0.04	0.30	0.08	0.06	0.123
H	0.14	0.04	0.20	0.06	0.111

occupied by alternatives B and F, i.e. the programmes of ATES and GRI. This last case is particularly significant, seeing that the GRI system is able to reach the third position, thanks to its brilliant performance in the most important criterion.

The AHP model has allowed us to better clarify the main attributes and to underline the advantages and the weaknesses of each programme. A consultation of the final and even partial rankings not only gives an overall judgement of the systems, it also indicates how each reporting scheme relates to the decision criteria. For example, the priorities for the first criterion show if and how the programme covers each of the three dimensions of responsibility. The operator is therefore provided with all the information necessary to come to a decision that responds perfectly to their needs. Thanks to the model, they are able to discover that the most effective programmes are those of ATT, ATES, and GRI. If for instance the operator has a small enterprise, he can choose to opt for the system of ATES, which is more suitable than the others, according to the weight obtained in criterion 2.

6. Conclusion and implications

The paper has first of all clarified the concepts of responsible tourism and CSR, given the proliferation of definitions that can create confusion and misunderstanding. Responsible tourism and CSR applied in tourism companies represent different concepts: on the one hand, a new way in which tourists conceive their holidays and to which the tourism industry has to answer with products alternative to mass tourism; on the other hand, a new business code of conduct, integrated by companies in all their processes and activities, in order to be more responsible towards society and the environment. Despite this difference, both responsible tourism and CSR bring enterprises to voluntarily behave in a more correct and ethical way towards tourists, society, and the environment, contributing to economic development, community well-being, and sustainable development.

The spread of responsible tourism and CSR in the tourism industry has generated the need for businesses to adopt systems for evaluating and certifying their commitment and responsibility from an environmental, social, and economic point of view. For this reason, the study, after underlining the meaning and significance of responsible tourism and CSR, has focussed on the analysis of the most important assessment systems of company responsibility. The paper has stressed that there are a lot of different reporting systems. The first important element of differentiation, which influences the other main attributes, is represented by the approach; some systems follow the "responsible tourism approach", assessing and certifying if a package holiday can be considered a responsible tourism product, while other systems are based on the "certification approach", focusing on the internal processes and CSR of the company. The other attributes of assessing programmes depend on the perspective followed: systems can give different attention to the environ-mental, social, and economic dimensions and they can be adopted by all companies or only by those who are specialized in responsible tourism. The study has also highlighted that if the programme is too complex and expensive, SMEs can find great difficulty in adopting and applying it.

After a qualitative analysis, we have used a quantitative model in order to clarify the main attributes, the strengths, and the weaknesses of the programmes and to offer more detailed and transparent information to tourism operators. We have chosen the AHP model, which, following a multi-criteria approach, compares and evaluates the performance of different alternatives with respect to a set of criteria, recognizing the best solutions. This model has allowed us to obtain an overall judgement of the effectiveness of programmes, after evaluating and comparing them with respect to different parameters. Thanks to the final and partial rankings, it is possible to define the best systems that satisfy decisional criteria better than the others and which are effective in evaluating company responsibility. The final results can represent some useful information for guiding tour operators in deciding what methodologies they can adopt and apply, according to their needs and size.

In spite of the advantages of the AHP model, there are some issues that need to be taken into consideration. First, the high number of criteria and programmes can make the procedure complex and time consuming and even impact negatively on the evaluation consistency. The second problem connected to the AHP model arises from the fact that every time a new alternative is added, all the evaluations need to be revised, even when the programmes that have already been considered have not been modified in any way. All the paired comparisons have to be made again and the weights of all the alternatives have to be recalculated. The reason is obviously linked to the procedure on which the AHP model is based, in that the priorities are determined by comparing each option with all the others, i.e. making relative comparisons, not absolute assessments. The third critical aspect is represented by the fact that AHP is a compensatory model in the sense that high priorities in some criteria can balance and compensate the weaknesses in other parameters. As a consequence, a system which is lacking with respect to one or more variables can, however, obtain a good position in the final ranking if it is excellent with respect to the other criteria. As a result, it is necessary to also consider carefully the partial ranking when choosing a system.

In spite of these critical aspects, the application of the AHP model has provided useful guidelines for tourism companies engaged in assessing their CSR and responsible tourism products. The study can indeed be considered as a tool aimed at supporting operators in assuming and evaluating their business responsibilities, while at the same time, offering sufficient guarantees to their consumers and the community at large. The proposal would be a starting point for putting into action effective and concrete measures to encourage the spread of responsible tourism and CSR and to stimulate the process by which tourism enterprises take on board their business responsibilities.

Notes

1. Email: ming@unive.it
2. Email: ericamin@unive.it

References

Akama, J.S., & Kieti, D. (2007). Tourism and socioeconomic development in developing countries: A case study of Mombasa Resort in Kenya. *Journal of Sustainable Tourism, 15*(6), 735–748.

Anderek, K.L., Valentine, K.M., Vogt, C.A., & Knopf, R.C. (2007). A cross cultural analysis of tourism and quality of life perceptions. *Journal of Sustainable Tourism, 5*(15), 483–582.

Bien, A. (2008). A simple user's guide to certification for sustainable tourism and ecotourism. *CESD Handbook, n.1*. Retrieved form http://www.responsibletravel.org/resources/certification-reports. html.

Commission of the European Communities (2001). Promoting a European Framework for Coporate Social Responsibility. COM (2001) 366 final. Retrieved from http://eurlex.eurpa.eu/LexUri Serv/site/en/com/2011 0366 en 01.pdf

Costa, P., Manente, M., & Furlan, M.C. (2001). *Politica economica del turismo*. TUP: Touring Editore, Milano.

Del Chiappa, G., Grappi, S., & Romani, S. (2009). The responsible tourist's behavior: An empirical analysis in Italy, January, Paper presented at the 8th International Congress Marketing Trends, Paris, France.

Dodds, R., & Joppe, M. (2005). *CSR in the tourism industry? The status of and potential for certification, codes of conduct and guidelines. CSR practice.* Washington, DC: Foreign Investment Advisory Service Investment Climate Department, IFC/ World Bank.

Ermlich, G. (2009). Corporate social responsibility (CSR). ITB, April. Paper presented at ITB Berlin.

Franch, M., Sambri, C., Martini, U., Pegan, G. & Rizzi, G. (2008). La domanda di turismo responsabile e di ecoturismo in Italia. Un'indagine esplorativa sui turisti CTS. Paper presented at the 6th International Congress of Marketing Trends. Venice, Italy.

Fuchs, H., Giraldo, A., Koschwitz, G., Loew, T. and Pfeifer, R. (2008). *Guidelines CSR - Reporting in Tourism.* Stuttgart: UWS Papier & Druck GmbH.

Goodwin, H. (2005). Responsible tourism and the market. *International Centre for Responsible Tourism, Occasional Paper, n. 4,* November.

GRI (2002). Tour operators' sector supplement. For use with the GRI 2002 sustainability reporting guidelines. Retrieved from http://www.globalreporting.org

Kalish, A. (2002). *Corporate futures. Social responsibility on the tourism industry.* London: Tourism Concern.

Kasim, A. (2006). The need of business environmental and social responsibility in the tourism industry. *International Journal of Hospitality & Tourism Administration, 7*(1), 1–22.

Kerala Declaration on Responsible Tourism (2008). Presented at 2nd International Conference on Responsible Tourism in Destinations – Kerala, India, March. Retrieved from http://www.res ponsibletourism2008.org/keraladeclaration.php

Manente, M., & Minghetti, V. (2010). Overview of methodologies for the analysis of responsible tourism and of CSR and proposal for a common EU responsibility label., CISET, EARTH. Retrieved from http://www.earth-net.eu/

Miller, G. (2001). Corporate Responsibility in the UK tourism industry. *Tourism Management, 22,* 589–598.

Responsible Travel Handbook (2006). Retrieved from http://www.transitionsabroad.com

Saaty, T.L. (1990a). *Decision making for leader: The analytic hierarchy process for decisions in a complex world.* Pittsburgh, PA: University of Pittsburgh.

Saaty, T.L. (1990b). *The analytic hierarchy process: Planning, priority setting, resources allocation.* Pittsburgh, PA: RWS publications.

Villagrán, D., Rodriguez, A., Benjumeda, I., Alarcón, P., Galindo, J., Pulido Arrebola, F.J., & Palomo, S. (2010). *Parámetros para medición de un turismo responsable* [Parameters for assessing responsible tourism]. Quidamtur S.L.L. & University of Málaga, Málaga.

World Business Council for Sustainable Development (1999). Meeting changing expectations: Corporate social responsibility. Retrieved from http://www.wbcsd.org/templates/Tem plateWBCSD5/layout.asp?type=p&MenuId=MTE0OQ

Knowledge transfer among clustered firms: a study of Brazil

Ariani Raquel Neckel Prux Stacke[a], Valmir Emil Hoffmann[b] and Helena Araujo Costa[b]

[a]Universidade para o Desenvolvimento do Alto Vale do Itajaí–Rua Guilherme Gemballa, 13, Caixa Postal 193, CEP: 89.160-000, Rio do Sul, SC, Brazil; [b]Universidade de Brasília – UnB, PPGA – Instituto Central de Ciências, Ala Norte, Subsolo, Módulo 25, 70910-900, Brasília, DF, Brazil

This paper analyses knowledge transfer among clustered firms and its relation to the competitiveness of a tourism destination in southern Brazil. It is assumed that knowledge is a strategic resource transferred among clustered firms. Research methods used were secondary data analysis followed by a survey conducted with 49 respondents. Findings show that the access to resources is more evident for the third sector and public administration than to firms. Besides, it was found that the knowledge transfer happens in different ways, but especially through the periodic meetings among the tourism firms. It was demonstrated that there is a better access and communication and information exchange among tourist firms, but the data have not connected knowledge transfer to destination competitiveness.

1. Introduction

The search for competitiveness has been the keynote of innumerable discussions during the last decade. According to Fensterseifer and Wilk (2003), there are a significant number of studies in this area, which have sought to understand the factors that influence the performance variations of firms, industries, regions, and nations. These studies are based on two different viewpoints. The first prioritizes an analysis of the external environment, based on studies carried out by Porter (1986, 1989). Yet, according to the second viewpoint and upon which this study is based, Barney (1991), Espino-Rodriguez and Gil-Padilha (2005), and Prahalad and Hamel (1990) all associate competitiveness with the internal resources accumulated by organizations. The basis of the competitive advantage within this last perspective resides in the access and/or the control of resources that possess certain characteristics, such as being rare, valuable, imperfectly imitable, and/or irreplaceable (Barney, 1991; Wernerfelt, 1984).

This research kept its focus on the strategic resources used by clustered firm organizations to generate competitive advantage, including inter-organizational relationships and knowledge. Clustered firms and other social actors promote the exchange of knowledge and strengthen cooperation among them. The first author to explain this issue was Alfred Marshall, who described how geographic concentration transforms the economy of a region (1982) and how the cluster can provide benefits for the firms and their business environment. Porter (1989) retrieved the term *cluster* which, according to him, refers to the idea of similar firms clustered together geographically and which are related or complementary to one another, thereby confirming the pioneer concept proposed by Marshall (1982).

Within a cluster, the sharing and/or access to resources can also be a source of competitive advantage for clustered firms in relation to outsiders (Hoffmann, Molina-Morales, & Martinez-Fernandez, 2011). In this context, it is possible to highlight the flow of knowledge that is also seen as a strategic resource (Grant, 1996; Prahalad & Hamel, 1990). Here, the cluster perspective is applied to the tourism sector since the destinations may be understood as a cluster firm. In addition, the use of this theoretical approach to research carried out in the tourism sector is still very recent and found in a few scientific research work as Breda, Costa and Costa (2006), Buhalis and Costa (2005), Hoffmann and Costa (2008), and Tinsley and Lynch (2001).

It may be perceived that there are several ways that knowledge transfer can occur within a cluster which are as follows: when there is interchange between actors, cooperation, interchange of workers (Brusco, 1993), social–cultural relationships (Hoffmann et al., 2011), support institutions (Brusco, 1993), and a mobile labour force (Cohen & Levinthal, 1990). For the discussion of this paper, the studies carried out by Priestley (n.d.) are of particular interest. A similar approach was applied to the tourist sector by Scott, Baggio, and Cooper (2008a). However, the authors showed that there was little discussion of this subject in tourism literature, in spite of the fact that the formulation, dissemination, and application of new information are crucial to developing innovations in this sector (Scott, Baggio, & Cooper, 2008b).

In a few words, this paper aims to evaluate knowledge transfer between clustered firms and its relationship to the competitiveness of the tourism destination of Urubici in the State of Santa Catarina, Brazil. Urubici was chosen for this investigation because it is part of a very unique tourism itinerary in Brazil, and popular due to the fact that it is the one of the few places in Brazil where snows every year. Urubici has a tourist potential represented by differential attractions (Government of Santa Catarina State Tourism Organization – Santur, 2006), that are still being developed but are already noteworthy because of the number of natural attractions that make this one of the principle ecotourism centres in the State.

In addition to this introduction, this article contains further four sections; Section 2 discusses knowledge and inter-organizational relationships, which is the theoretical basis of this work; Section 3 presents the methodology used; Section 4 contains an analysis of the final results; and Section 5 presents the conclusions, limitations, and possibilities for future researches.

2. Knowledge transfer and inter-organizational relations among clustered firms

According to Mamberti and Braga (2004), the geographic space is one of the most important specificities in the social practice of tourism. In this sense, Petrocchi (2001) states that a tourism activity grows around tourism attractions, regardless of the fact that they are in natural, historic, urban, and cultural or leisure areas, and end up leading to cluster the firms, very often quite naturally. Thus, in tourism, most products "are constructed in well-defined geographic environments, where activities are developed that constitute the process of production" (Beni, 2004, p. 154).

Cluster (Porter, 1989), *industrial district* (Becattini, 1990; Brusco, 1993), and *local productive arrangements* (Lastres & Cassiolato, 2005) among others are the terms that give weight to the notion of clustered firms and give a sense of direction to the search for competitiveness by means of a type of industrial organization. Although this study recognizes the different concepts mentioned, it adopts the notion of clustered firms, since this is a common characteristic in all these conceptualizations. The main ideas that firms and institutions that are territorially close can generate affinities and interactions (Porter, 1989) and propitiate the creation of inter-organizational networks (Hoffmann et al., 2011). In such types of interactions, it is possible to have knowledge transfer, either tactic or explicit. Such resources shared by the cluster firms will only generate competitive advantages if the access and/or control of resources are greater within the firms in relation to the outside companies (Hoffmann et al., 2011).

The definition that Porter (1991, p. 211) gave to cluster firms may be transferred to an analysis of tourism clusters, even though the author does not work specifically in this sector. In his opinion a cluster is: "[...] a concentrated geographic grouping of inter-related companies, institutions correlated in a determined area linked by common and complimentary elements". Porter (1991) also explains that in a place such a cluster frequently exist cooperation and competition at same time. Firms cooperate each other to solve common problems, like workforce training, but competition is maintained, in the sense of products and or markets.

Various studies highlight clustering as an important factor for sharing or generating resources, in which knowledge is included (Amato, 2000; Ebers & Jarillo, 1998; Lastres & Cassiolato, 2005; Song, Wong, & Chon, 2003). For Song et al. (2003), in closed environments, where there are strategic alliances among the social players, there will be a sharing of resources with the overall objective of winning competitive advantages. In addition, Marshall (1982, p. 234) described the advantage of being part of a cluster of firms was that "if one launches a new idea, it is immediately adopted by the others, who come together with their own suggestions and the idea thereby becomes a source of new ideas".

One of the necessary factors for sharing some resources is the existence of cooperation between the companies. Inter-organizational cooperation can encourage companies to meet needs that they would otherwise be unable to do with an isolated action. The cooperation happens in different forms such as the sharing of a qualified labour force, collective purchasing of raw materials and specialized services, access to new markets, as well as the transfer of knowledge (Hoffmann & Costa, 2008).

Knowledge itself can be shared in several different ways among companies within the cluster, according to Molina-Morales, López-Navarro, and Guia-Julve (2001). This transfer varies from a more structured model to informal methods (Scott et al., 2008b), and can occur through the interactions outside the firm that allow a continual transmission of ideas, or through the mobility of the labour force. Thus, the employees, when they change companies, end up taking tacit knowledge with them which they acquired in the firm where they worked as stated by Cohen and Levinthal (1990). For Molina-Morales et al. (2001), the previous experience of employees who have already worked in the region, and in the same sector of industry, is very positive and makes it possible for them to begin their activities rapid and with less need of adaptation. Highly qualified employees can also obtain access to outside knowledge, either through research, by participating in events, or from others (Cohen & Levinthal, 1990).

Inter-organizational relationships, in turn, also bring the possibility of resources sharing, including knowledge, as focused in this study. According to Claro, Claro, and Hagelaar (2002), these are maintained and explored through social contacts and events that previously involved implicit motives, such as the exchange of information and experiences. Another point within the clusters is related to the support institutions, which offer specific support services of a non-financial nature to the companies (Brusco, 1993), and which can also provide other resources. They operate as knowledge and opportunities repositories with regard to innovation (Molina-Morales & Hoffmann, 2002). Under a network analysis perspective, they are called a "structural hole" (Burt, 2004), which reinforces contact between groups, as well as the search for alternatives and innovation.

When studying how cluster firms create knowledge, Malmberg and Power (2005) analysed three models: first, knowledge in clusters is created through various forms of local inter-organizational collaborative interaction and can be done through the interaction of actors involved in business, or through the ties of cooperation and partnership between the companies and development institutes. This can also be done through high-level competition and intense rivalry. In this context, for Malmberg and Power (2005), rivalry is a key factor and driving force for business entrepreneurs and is a useful tool. Brusco (1993) highlights the existence of support institutions for the knowledge flow. According to Molina-Morales and Hoffmann (2002), knowledge transfer occurs also through such institutions, in the form of social–cultural relations and cooperation, which leads one to analyse the role and importance of institutions within the cluster. In a few words, they are taken as company associations, technological institutes, governmental agencies, public, and private sources of financing.

According to Nakano (2005), some of the factors that can influence knowledge transfer involve the type of knowledge to be transferred and some characteristics of the network itself, such as its structure, the administrative capacity of the organization, and the trust that exists between its members. This relates also to the importance given to the reputation of the companies involved. Teece, Pisano, and Schuen (1997) wrote that reputation is seen as a resource that, within a cluster, can reduce behavioural uncertainties between the companies and even provide information with respect to trust (Jones, Hesterley, & Borgartti, 1997). Thus, the following may be considered to be a summary of the ways that knowledge may be transferred between cluster firms: cooperation between companies; the mobility of the labour force; support institutions, inter-relations between members, and research. More specifically for this study, knowledge transfer will be observed through the cooperation that exists between companies, support institutions, and the inter-relationship between members and information.

3. Methodology

This research was carried out in two stages. The first was secondary data collection from documents, promotional material, and electronic sites. In this first stage, written questions were sent to the City Secretary of Tourism. The objective was to seek information about the tourism activity in the area, and this was done by means of a questionnaire that was sent by e-mail, containing open questions. The second stage consisted on a survey. The variables, already valid, are presented in Figure 1. A semantic scale of seven points was used, where the number one (01) representing low intensity and seven (07) indicating high intensity of accordance.

The list of 54 interviewees was based on the information provided by the Secretariat Tourism in Urubici (2006). This included the names and addresses of the actors involved in tourism activities in private, public, and third sectors. A pre-test was conducted by one representative from each sector in order to identify and eliminate potential problems (Malhotra, 2006) in the research instrument.

All potential interviewees were contacted. In total, 49 respondents participated in this research: 81.63% (40 people) were from the private sector, 12.24% (six people) were from the public sector, and 6.12% (three people) represented NGO. It should be noted that there

Constructs*	Variables	Reference authors
1) Resources availability	- existence; - use; - relationship	Barney (1991); Molina-Morales, Guia & Lopez (2001); Song, Wong & Chong (2003)
2) Support Institutions Survey with closed questions. Semantic scale (1 to down and 7 to high)	Importance	Brusco(1993); Priestley (n.d.); Esser et al (1994); Molina-Morales & Hoffmann (2002)
3) Firm relationships	- relationship -localization - interchange information - Information access and availability	Prahalad & Hamel (1990); Nonaka & Takeuchi (1997); Malmberg & Power (2005)
4) Competitiveness	- cooperation, trust and communication - number of tourists Firm knowledge about tourists and their spendings; Jobs, training and paid salary	Prahalad & Hamel (1990); Espino-Rodriguez & Gil-Padilla (2005); Riveiro & Caldeira (2004)

Figure 1. Constructs, variables, authors, and instruments. *To constructs (1)–(3) instrument used was survey with closed questions with a semantic scale (1 to low intensity of agreement and 7 to high). To construct (4) instrument was a survey with closed questions with a nominal scale.

was one more respondent from the public sector. Based on this research, it was confirmed that the tourism and hotel businesses in this tourism destination were divided between: hotels, hostels, restaurants, tourist transfer firms, and entertainment centres. In order to analyse the data, quantitative methodological support was used. Both univaried analysis (a descriptive analysis based on the frequencies) and bivaried analysis were conducted.

Also, a factorial analysis was carried out in order to extract the principal components and the number of factors (Hair, Anderson, Tatham, & Black, 2005). The varimax rotation method was applied during the factor extraction. To extract the number of factors, the Kaiser criterion was used, which considers only the auto-values higher than 1, as being statistically significant. The load factor value was defined based on Hair et al. (2005) and was equal to or higher than 0.5. In order to carry out a comparative analysis, a parametric contrast measurement analysis was used (test t), which made it possible to verify the significance of the differences in measurements between the private and public sectors. For the comparison, the public sector was merged with the third sector. The confidence interval used was 95% and the significance was assumed for values under 0.05. One last *cluster* type analysis was made among the companies participating in the study based on the factorial scores, which was implemented in accordance with the Ward method and Euclidean distances as described by Malhotra (2006). The linkage distance used to obtain the groups was in the value of 20, where a lower number of groups was obtained but which preserved a certain homogeneity between the factorial scores and the factors.

4. Results

The analysed tourism destination is one of the most promising ecotourism centres in the State of Santa Catarina[1], and its principal tourist attractions include its natural resources, the cold weather, and a range of outdoor activities. However, according to Souza (2005), until 1950, there was only one hostel in Urubici and its first restaurant opened in 1970. He further affirms that the most consistent tourist infrastructure began from 1992 to 1996. His research data show that 85% of all tourism organizations were created in a 10-year period (1996–2005).

The companies included in our study are mainly family-run business (92.5%), which started when the young sons and daughters left home and their bedrooms were rented out by the family. With regard to the public sector, it was seen that this is also a recent development. According to Souza (2005), during the period between 1992 and 1995, there began a conscious effort to install road signs in the town and at tourist points, tourist information centres were implanted and the capacity of the town's accommodation and gastronomic sector has increased. That is to say, the organization of this sector is recent; it started to be developed in the 1990s and has resulted in the creation of new enterprises.

In the municipality it was identified the Association of Urubici Hostels and Hotels – POUSERRA (*Associação das Pousadas e Hotéis de Urubici – POUSERRA*), founded in 2001, with the aim of interacting between the public authorities and the private sector to promote and develop tourism in the area. According to its President, meetings among associates take place once a month, in the home of one of them, and the aim of these meetings is to discuss difficulties and decide about promotional material, among others. In this way, cooperation, the exchange of information, and a collective spirit are developed and preserved by members of the Association.

4.1. Indicative factors of interorganizational relations and knowledge transfer

A factorial analysis determined three factors, which correspond to 50% of the total variance, which can be considered adequate, according to Hair et al. (2005)[2]:

  (a) Factor 1 – access to resource and relationships;
  (b) Factor 2 – the importance of the institutions;
  (c) Factor 3 – information exchange.

Considering the resources are tangible or intangible assets linked to the company (Barney, 1991), there are many ways to access them (Molina-Morales et al., 2001; Song et al., 2003; Teece et al., 1997). In this study, access to resources (Factor 1) that were made available to the destination by the sectors involved may be observed in Table 1.

Table 2 presents the importance of institutions (Factor 2) under the perspective of both groups. It is noteworthy to see that the companies, the private groups, and the public authority considering to be easy to establish social relationships with their competitors, since the highest averages were given to this question and the standard deviation for both sectors was lower than the rest. When these are compared, it may be deduced that the private groups and the public authority presented a higher average than the companies.

Table 1. Test *t* for Factor 1 – access to resource and relationships.

Indicators	Companies				NGO and the public sector				
	Average	Mode	Median	SD	Average	Mode	Median	SD	Test *t*
E5 – privileged access to resources	3.35	1e4	3.50	1.833	4.78	6	6	1.986	0.043*
E6 – facility to establish social relations with competitors	4.73	5	5	1.710	6.33	7	7	1.000	0.009*
E15 – services and support to R&D are supplied by the institutions	3.48	1	3.48	1.961	5	6	6	2.179	0.044*
E16 – utilizes the services provided by the institutions	3.35	1	3	2.214	5.11	4	5	1.453	0.009*
E37 – a strong relationship exists between the institutions and the private groups	3.65	1	3	2.131	4.11	4e5	4	1.764	0.549

*$p < 0.05$.

Table 2. Test *t* for Factor 2 – the importance of the institutions.

Indicators	Companies				NGO and the public sector				Test *t*
	Average	Mode	Median	SD	Average	Mode	Median	SD	
E14 – research and teaching institutions are important	6.13	7	7	1.488	5.67	6	6	1.118	0.390
E17d – government is important	5.08	7	6	2.235	7	7	7	0.000	0.000*
E17b – tourism firms (TF) are important for tourism in town	6.43	7	7	1.059	6.78	7	7	0.667	0.346
E17 h – associations and unions are important	5.53	7	7	1.853	6.56	7	7	1.014	0.031*

*$p < 0.05$.

Consonant with Factor 1, and also present in Factor 3 – which presents the information exchange among the interviewees (Table 3), the institutions and government realize that there is more information exchange among the companies than with themselves, with averages significantly higher in four of the five variables. The only exception was related to products and services, shown in the centre of the scale for both groups. It may be noted that the companies believe their information exchange has an average rate with a response bias towards the lower end of the scale, while the institutions and government both indicated values with a higher scale bias.

Figure 2 presents the *cluster* analysis made for the group of companies, taking into account the factorial scores. Table 4 shows four clusters in their specificities, that is to say, based on the questions represented by the respective factors from the sum total of the averages. This made it possible to carry out an analysis of the perception of each group in respect to each factor.

4.2. *Discussion*

Based on the results regarding Factor 2, there is a different evaluation between the two groups (companies vs. public authority and the NGO). While the second showed values between the central point and above, the first indicated most values below the central point of the scale. Based on this difference, it may be considered, though with the risk of making a certain value judgment, that the opinions of the companies are more important since they are, after all, the main beneficiaries of such resources. This particular risk is lessened by the fact that most literature related to resources understand companies as an analysis unit, for example, as in the case of Barney (1991), Peteraf (1993), and Wernerfelt (1984). If, on the one hand, companies obtain competitive advantage on the basis of the scarcity and/or the unavailability of resources to others, by not having access to such resources, they will also be unable to obtain this advantage themselves. In this sense, emerges the first proposition from this result:

Proposition 1:   Different kind of actors present in a tourism cluster may have different perception about resources availability.

Within the variables that compose Factor 1, *E3 – the facility to establish social relations with competitors*, certainly deserves a mention. In the text by Molina-Morales et al. (2001), a cluster is taken as an industrial district and this in turn as a community of people. Various studies that deal with the theme highlight this aspect in particular. When dealing with tourism, Mamberti and Braga (2004) wrote that a geographical space is linked to social practices; whereas Malmberg and Power (2005) emphasized that a cluster can promote the interaction between agents. This means that this variable has assumed greater importance in the analysis, since it was the one that was given the best evaluation by the companies; which seems to confirm the references that were used that deal with interaction between actors in the context of a cluster.

This importance may be verified principally in relation to the fact that interaction leads to an indirect exchange of knowledge; we mean that which occurs in an informal manner, in an environment that is different to a professional one, but which is equally propitious for exchanges of this type, including, for instance, those of a social nature. Returning to Marshall (1982), in a sense these environments enable specific knowledge to 'hover in the air'.

In accordance to the literature that has been reviewed, it is known that access to resources can be a competitive advantage for the companies (Barney, 1991; Peteraf, 1993;

Table 3. Test *t* for Factor 3 – information exchange.

Indicators	Companies				NGO and the public sector				Test *t*
	Average	Mode	Median	SD	Average	Mode	Median	SD	
E11 – there is an informal transfer of innovation and knowledge between the TF	4.30	5	4.50	1.843	5.56	5	5	1.333	0.060*
E18 – institutional information about products and services is available	3.23	1	2.224	2.224	5.56	5e6	6	1.236	0.000*
E21 – interchange of information about products and services between TF	4.10	4	4	1.516	4.56	3e6	5	1.810	0.435
E22 – interchange of information about markets and clients among TF	4.05	4	4	1.739	5.33	5e7	5	1.581	0.048*
H27 – regular meetings are held	4.35	7	5	2.119	5.33	5e6	5	1	0.047*

*p < 0.05.

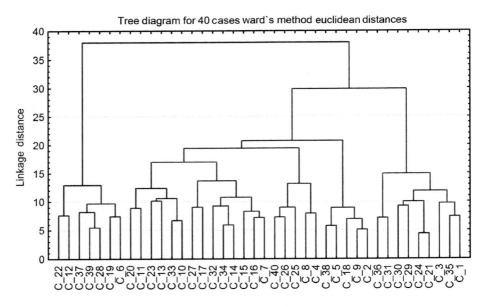

Figure 2.   Tree diagram obtained from the cluster analysis.

Wernerfelt, 1984). In Urubici, it was generally seen that access to resources is still restricted, but it was perceived that social relationships between the competitors are one of the ways that the companies, private groups, and public authorities have to access the existing resources in this destination. In this case, it is possible to add that an increase or loss of competitiveness depends on the intensity of the relationship with the other social agents (Silva, 2004). In this specific analysis, this may be seen to be a positive aspect. So a second proposition is designed:

Proposition 2:   Indirect interaction among actors in a tourism cluster can lead to an indirect knowledge exchange.

In Factor 2, the importance of the support institutions is of particular interest, since the institutions are essential due to their capacity to provide services in a more focused way and at a lower price. Another reason is the ability that these institutions have to capture externally and internalize relevant information within the clusters (Brusco, 1993). Table 2 shows that, in spite of the fact that the institutions and the public authority have again awarded a higher value to almost all of the variables, the biased response of the researchers is high. This observation is important for an analysis within a cluster since, in accordance

Table 4.   Average values of the groups obtained from the clusters analysis in relation to the factors.

	F1 resources	F2 institutions	F3 information exchange
New average value	20	16	20
Group 1 (7 cases)	29.71 (+)	26.57 (+)	26.42 (+)
Group 2 (19 cases)	18.42 (−)	24.63 (+)	22 (+)
Group 3 (5 cases)	10.4 (−)	26.6 (+)	12.4 (−)
Group 4 (9 cases)	14.66 (−)	15.44 (−)	15.11 (−)

Observation: The pointers between brackets correspond to higher (+) or lower (−) scores in relation to the sum total of the scale.

with Porter (1989), its members are mutually dependent on each other and the good performance of one can increase the success of the others. Therefore, it is necessary that companies and support institutions perceive their importance, so as to stimulate activity, especially because the tourism destination is formed by several agents who, informally grouped, seek to offer their clients competitive advantages (Toledo, Valdes, & Pollero, 2003). This is something that can be underlined in Urubici, since both the public and private sectors state that they understand the importance of the institutions.

For Priestley (n.d.), interaction between economic, social–cultural, political, and institutional actors increases knowledge and the ability to change their behaviour, finding new solutions in response to change. This statement seems relevant, since this research study verified knowledge transfer in the tourism destination and, as seen here, the actors are recognized as being important within the cluster being studied, which can result in the transfer of knowledge. Moreover, according to Esser, Hillebrabd, Messener, and Meyer-Stamer (1994), competitiveness emerges through the participation and the complex and dynamic interaction between the different actors. More specifically in tourism, competitiveness depends on the experiences of the tourists as a whole, who are satisfied by having available a greater selection of services and that this whole series of positive experiences will only occur if there is cooperation between the public and private sectors (Dias, 2003).

In spite of the discrepancies between the answers given by the different sectors, this question attained high averages, showing that the different tourism sectors are important in the tourism destination. In addition, it was seen that support institutions are also understood to be important for the development of tourist activities, particularly in Urubici. With regard to information exchange, this can occur by means of interaction between actors within the cluster network (Balestrin, Vargas, & Fayard, 2005; Malmberg & Power, 2005). Based on that, two propositions are presented:

Proposition 3: Institutions in a tourism cluster are important to develop a competitive advantage.

Proposition 4: Institutions are direct and or indirect connected to knowledge transfer among clustered tourism firms.

It is therefore understood that an organization cannot create knowledge without the initiative of the individual and the interaction that occur within the group. Knowledge may be enhanced or crystallized at group level through discussion, the sharing of experiences, and observations (Nonaka & Takeuchi, 1997).

These results means that it can be acknowledged that there is an information exchange between the companies, but that this is probably being carried out at medium intensity. In the case of the companies, none of the values rose higher than the centre of the scale, except for the question related to the availability of institutional information about products and services, which is a precise reference to the role of the institutions present in the cluster. Since this variable assumes a response bias that appears to be paradoxical, this was where the greatest differences existed between the two groups of respondents. Going back to a theoretical perspective, it is understood that information may be exchanged in different ways among the companies that form the cluster, and that this can occur by means of interactions that take place outside the company which permit a continual transmission of ideas (Molina-Morales et al., 2001). In Urubici, this interaction also occurs through regular meetings among the local tourism organizations, which make it possible to exchange information.

Claro et al. (2002) support that resources may be transferred through social contacts and events that involve motives that were previously seen to be implicit, such as exchanging information and experiences. Therefore, this study shows that there is knowledge transfer in Urubici, including meetings held by tourism companies, as well as the exchange of information, as seen from the point of view of the companies. However, the public sector indicates that there are various types of interaction that permits the transfer of knowledge, in particular the availability of institutional information about products and services. The data also show that knowledge transfer tends to occur within the sectors themselves and not between sectors; that is to say, it is clear that private companies transfer more information between themselves than they do with the public sector. This inference may be made, when the indicators that reflect the relationship between the public and private sectors are analysed. So, our next proposition is about:

Proposition 5: Knowledge transfer is not necessary equal among different groups or sectors in a tourism cluster.

The cluster analysis can be seen on Table 4, where it is perceived that it was found four groups. Group 1, which includes seven cases, was the only one to consider all above average values and have a positive view about the factors that were found in this analysis. Regarding their particularities, it should be highlighted that 48.9% have secondary education and 28.6% hold postgraduation certificates. Meanwhile, the management of these companies is 100% family-based, of which 71.4% were inaugurated between 2000 and 2006, and that 71.4% are guest houses or hostels.

Group 2 includes 19 cases. This, in turn, gave two high averages to F2 (INST) and F3 (TRANS). As a characteristic, it should be highlighted that only one business venture is managed professionally, the others are all family-based concerns of which 63.2% are guest houses or hostels; 31.6% are restaurants, and 5.3% are reception companies. Only 15.8% of the companies belong to POUSERRA, this being the group with the lowest level of participation in the Association.

Group 3 consists of five cases, which answered only Factor 2 (INST) of the questionnaire, with a higher than average value. With regard to their specificities, it was noted that this group is the most diversified and has the smaller number of guest houses/hostels, only 20% of the total, but in compensation has the largest number of hotels (40%). These companies also represent the most recent of the business ventures; 80% were inaugurated between 2003 and 2005, which corroborates information from the first group, and management is 100% family-based. What is of particular interest is the fact that 40% of these enterprises participate in the municipal Association – POUSERRA, since this group represents the largest number of associates.

Group 4 includes nine cases, and is highlighted because it has the greatest diversity of establishments and because most of these are concentrated in the restaurant business, with 55% of the total. Another important characteristic is the participation of an entertainment company; Group 4 was the only group to consider this type of participation, the remaining enterprises that are part of this group are all hotels and guest houses/hostels. Thus, it was seen that various branches of tourist activities are inserted within this group.

This group is also characterized for owning the oldest companies, 33.3% of these were inaugurated between 1988 and 1989. The majority of the management, 55.5%, have completed third-grade education and 22.2% are postgraduates. This variable makes it possible to suggest that this group has the highest percentage of managers with higher education. With regard to the management of these business enterprises, this is presented in three forms: family-based, professional, and mixed, and that this is the only group with this particular characteristic. It should also be mentioned that, in the three factors and in its sum total, this group obtained the lowest of the average values.

Cluster type analysis noted that among the four groups presented only one attained a higher value for all factors. Showing that it conducts its business in a positive way, the greater part of this group is composed of guest houses with family-based management and that most of the business ventures were inaugurated during an interval of 6 years (2000– 2006). In contrast, the group that presented a less higher than average value, Group 4, consisting of nine cases, with specificities that concentrate on diversity within the existing segments of this group, in that 55.6% are restaurants and own the oldest business establishments, and are the only ones that have various forms of management (family-based, professional, and mixed). Therefore, it may be concluded that few differences were found between the groups, which makes this analysis all the more difficult.

5. Conclusion and implications

The aim of this study was to evaluate the knowledge transfer of among clustered firms in the tourism destination of Urubici, situated in the state of Santa Catarina, Brazil. For this, a quantitative research method was used.

For this study, definitions from Barney (1991) are of particular interest for an analysis, since it is possible to see that competitive advantage refers to the capacity of a tourism destination to use its resources efficiently (Riveiro & Caldera, 2004), in that the members of a cluster are mutually dependent upon each other and that the good performance of one can increase the success of the others (Porter, 1989). The opportunity that the tourism destinations have in sharing their resources to obtain competitive advantage, as opposed to those who do not form part of the cluster, has also been ascertained. Based on the type of resource that may be present in a tourism destination; that is to say, cooperation, trust, knowledge, innovation, and others, it was concluded that tourism has characteristics that are similar to manufacturing industries.

In this research, these resources originated three factors in the explanatory phase. It can be concluded that, among the three factors found, the one that may be considered as a strategic resource is that which deals with institutions from the point of view of the companies. Factor 1, access to resources and relationships, shows that the private groups and public authority assign a higher average to this question than the companies.

With regard to the importance of support institutions in the tourism destination, it is noted that this variable received averages above the central point of the scale, which shows a tendency towards agreement. This resource illustrated the importance of the different actors in the tourist destination. This seemed to be a positive factor in favour of Urubici since, in accordance with Silva (2004), support institutions are essential to the process of development and to strengthen tourist activities, which can generate a competitive advantage for the destination. Regarding information exchange, it was seen that the companies transfer knowledge through social relations as, for example, regular meetings.

With regard to the results described in Factors 1 and 2, certain differences were noted. In the first, the companies claimed that it was easier to establish social relationships with their competitors than it was with institutions and private groups. When asked about the importance of the different segments, including these, the average given was higher. Another factor of perception that the companies have in relation to the institutions and associations is that, although they stated that these were important, they also described how services, such as research and development (R&D), were unavailable. This must have been noted by the managers, since this service is being carried out, but is not accessible to the companies. When specifically analysing the creation of knowledge in a cluster, Malmberg and Power (2005) defend the idea that the partnership between the companies and the development institutes is an important factor.

With regard to the exchange of information, based on the relationships among the companies, it was concluded that the tourism destination transfers knowledge resources by means of regular meetings and that, in the case of the public authority, an informal transfer of innovation and knowledge exists and that institutional information is also available. This result seems to be related to the practice of relationships between the companies that can be described as informal. Thus, there seems to be harmony between what is social practice and the exchange of information between actors.

When comparing the data from Factors 1 and 3, it was seen that there are divergences between the private and public sectors, since each one shows that it has better access to communication with actors from its own sector. This result might seem paradoxical since, while institutions are seen to be important, as all those involved in this research claimed almost unanimously, on the other hand, there seems to be a difficulty in establishing a network that has more inter-organizational characteristics. Finally, based on all the findings the paper leaded to five propositions:

1. Different kind of actors present in a tourism cluster may have different perception about resources availability.
2. Indirect interaction among actors in a tourism cluster can lead to an indirect knowledge exchange.
3. Institutions in a touristic cluster are important to develop a competitive advantage.
4. Institutions are direct and or indirect connected to knowledge transfer in a tourism cluster (or among clustered tourism firms?).
5. Knowledge transfer is not necessary equal among different groups or sectors in a tourism cluster.

This study raises several other questions. Another conclusion is that it seems that the private groups and local government give a more positive perspective upon the factors analysed. That is to say, in all the differences that were considered as being significant, the highest values, or rather those that expressed a more positive view, came from the companies and from the government. What does this mean? That they have a positive view because they do not know the companies well? That they are positively evaluating the tasks that they are responsible for themselves (availability of institutional information)? We believe there are insufficient elements in this research to answer these questions. For this reason, this is a path that can be followed in the future, when such an investigation can continue in a qualitative way. Another possibility would be to replicate this same study in other clusters, in order to identify the possibility of an idiosyncratic characteristic or otherwise in relation to these actors, and even to these same competitive resources.

Notes

1. http://www.urubici.com.br.
2. In order to simplify this, the variables are described in the corresponding comparative table.

References

Amato Neto, J. (2000). Redes de Cooperação Produtiva e Clusters Regionais: oportunidades para as pequenas e médias empresas. São Paulo: Atlas.

Balestrin, A., Vargas, L.M., & Fayard, P. (2005). Criação de conhecimento nas redes de cooperação interorganizacional. *Revista de Administração de Empresas, 45*, 53–65.

Barney, J. (1991). Firm resources and sustained (...). *Journal of Management*, 7(1), 99–120, doi: 10.1177/014920639101700108.

Becattini, G. (1990). The Marshallian industrial district as a socio-economic notion. In F. Pyke, G. Becattini, & W. Sengeberger (Eds.), *Industrial districts and local economic regeneration* (pp. 37–51). Geneva: International Institute for Labour Studies.

Beni, M. (2004). *Análise estrutural do turismo*. São Paulo: SENAC São Paulo.

Breda, Z.C., Costa, R., & Costa, C. (2006). Do clusters and networks make small places beautiful? In L. Lazzereti & C. Petrillo (Eds.), *Tourism local systems and networking* (pp. 67–82). Oxford: Elsevier.

Brusco, S. (1993). Pequeñas empresas y prestación de servicios reales. In F. Pyke & W. Sergenberger (Eds.), *Los DI y las PMYES: DI y Regeneración Económica Local* (pp. 235–258). Madrid: MSSS.

Buhalis, D., & Costa, C. (Eds.). (2005). *Tourism management dynamics*. London: Elsevier.

Burt, R.S. (2004). Structural holes and good Ideas. *American Journal of Sociology*, 110, 349–369.

Claro, D.P., Claro, P.B., & Hagelaar, G. (2002). Rede estratégica na seleção e na manutenção (...). *Revista de Administração*, 37, 6–18.

Cohen, W.M., & Levinthal, D.A. (1990). Absorptive capacity: New perspective on learning and innovation. *Administrative Science Quarterly*, 35, 128–152.

Dias, R. (2003). *Planejamento do turismo: política e desenvolvimento do turismo no Brasil*. São Paulo: Atlas.

Ebers, M., & Jarillo, J.C. (1998). Preface the construction, forms, and consequences of industry networks. *International Studies of Management and Organization*, 27, 3–21.

Espino-Rodríguez, T.F., & Gil-Padilha, A.M. (2005). Determinants of information systems outsourcing in hotels (...). *The International Journal of Tourism Research*, 7, 35–47.

Esser, K., Hillebrabd, W., Messener, D., & Meyer-Stamer, J. (1994). *Competitividad sistémica:* (...). Berlin: Instituto Alemán de Desarrolho.

Fensterseifer, J. Evaldo & Wilk, E.O. (2003). Visão da firma baseada em recursos, cluster e performance: um estudo no setor vitivnícola do RS. Paper presented at XXVII Encontro da Anpad, São Paulo.

Grant, R.M. (1996). Toward a knowledge-based theory (...). *Strategic Management Journal*, 17, 109–122.

Hair, J.F., Anderson, R.E., Tatham, R.L., & Black, W. (2005). *Análise multivariada de dados*. Porto Alegre: Bookman.

Hoffmann, V.E., & Costa, H.A. (2008). Competitividade Sistêmica em Destinos Turísticos. *Encontro da Anpad*, 32, no page.

Hoffmann, V.E., Molina-Morales, F.X., & Martínez-Fernández, M.T. (2011). Evaluation of competitiveness in ceramic. *European Business Review*, 23, 87–105.

Jones, C., Hesterley, W.S., & Borgartti, S.P.P. (1997). A general theory of network governance: (...). *Academy of Management Review*, 22, 911–945.

Lastres, H.M.M., & Cassiolato, J.E. (2005). *Mobilizando conhecimentos para desenvolver arranjos e sistemas produtivos* (...). Rio de Janeiro: Redesist.

Malhotra, N. (2006). *Pesquisa de marketing: uma orientação aplicada*. Porto Alegre: Bookman.

Malmberg, A., & Power, D. (2005). (How) do (firms in) clusters create knowledge? *Industry and Innovation*, 12, 409–431.

Mamberti, M.M.S., & Braga, R. (2004). Arranjos produtivos e desenvolvimento local., Paper presented at I Seminário Internacional o Desenvolvimento Local na Integração. Rio Claro.

Marshall, A. (1982). *Princípios da economia: tratado introdutório*. São Paulo: Abril.

Molina-Morales, F.X., López, M.A., & Guia, J. (2001). Social capital in territorial agglomerations of firms: Opportunities and restraints., Paper presented at 17th Conference of the EGOS. Lyon, France.

Molina-Morales, F.X. & Hoffmann, V. E. (2002). Aprendizagem através de redes sociais - O efeito da proximidade geográfica. Inteligência Empresarial (UFRJ), Rio de Janeiro, 12, pp. 4-11.

Nakano, D.N. (2005). Fluxos de conhecimento em redes interorganizacionais: conceitos e fatores de influência. In J. Amato Neto (Ed.), *Redes entre organizações: domínio do conhecimento e da eficácia operacional* (pp. 54–67). São Paulo: Atlas.

Nonaka, I., & Takeuchi, H. (1997). *Criação do conhecimento na empresa*. Rio de Janeiro: Campus.

Peteraf, M.A. (1993). The cornerstones of competitive advantage: A resource-based view. *Strategic Management Journal*, 14, 179–188.

Petrocchi, M. (2001). *Gestão de pólos turísticos.* São Paulo: Futuro.

Porter, M. (1986). *Estratégia competitiva:* (. . .). Rio de Janeiro: Campus.

Porter, M. (1989). *A vantagem competitiva das nações.* Rio do Janeiro: Campus.

Porter, M. (1991). *Competição: estratégias competitivas essenciais.* Rio de Janeiro: Campus.

Priestley, J.L. (n.d.). Knowledge transfer within interorganizational networks., M/D ideagroup-chapter.1.pdf, Kennesaw State University.

Prahalad, C.K., & Hamel, G. (1990). The core competence of the firm. *Harvard Business Review, 68,* 79–87.

Rivero, M.S., & Caldera, M.A. (2004). La competitividad de los destinos turísticos: un análise cuantitativo mediante modelos logísticos. Aplicación a los municipios extremenõs., Paper presented at I Jornada de Economia del Turismo, Palma de Mallorca.

Santur, Gerĕncia de Planejamento (2006). Perfil da demanda turística de Santa Catarina 2006. Available at http://santur.sc.gov.br (accessed 5 March 2006).

Scott, N., Baggio, R., & Cooper, C. (Eds.). (2008a). *Network analysis in tourism.* Clevedon: Channel View.

Scott, N., Baggio, R., & Cooper, C. (2008b). Tourism destination networks and knowledge transfer. In N. Scott, R. Baggio, & C. Cooper (Eds.), *Network analysis and tourism* (pp. 40–56). Clevedon: Channel View.

Secretaria Municipal de Indústria, Comércio e Turismo de Urubici (2006). *Tabela de fluxo de turistas.* Urubici.

Silva, T. (2004). Rede de cooperação entre pequenas empresas do setor turístico. *Passos Revista de Turismo y Patrimônio Cultural, 2,* 267–279.

Song, H., Wong, K., & Chon, K.K.S. (2003). Modelling and forecasting the demand for Hong Kong tourism. *Hospitality Management, 22,* 435–451.

Souza, A.M. (2005). Turismo na serra catarinense: um exercício de observação sobre a população do município de Urubici. *Turismo Visão e Ação, 7,* 387–398.

Teece, D.J., Pisano, G., & Shuen, A. (1997). Dynamics capabilities and strategic managenent. *Strategic Management Jounal, 18,* 509–533.

Tinsley, R., & Lynch, P. (2001). Small tourism businesses networks and destination development. *International Journal of Hospitality Management, 20*(4), 367–378.

Toledo, G.L., Álvarez-Valdéz, J., & Pollero, Á.C. (2003). Configuración del turismo em el Ambiente globalizado. *Turismo em Análise, 13*(1), 94–104.

Wernerfelt, B. (1984). A resource-based view of the firm. *Strategic Management Journal, 5,* 171–180.

Business format franchise in regional tourism development

Wojciech Czakon

Faculty of Management, University of Economics in Katowice, ul. Bogucicka 14, Katowice 40-226, Poland

Tourism becomes increasingly an industry where interorganizational relationships can provide a global competitive advantage (Porter, 1990). Collaborative relationships are in focus for three decades now, yet interorganizational literature findings have been criticized (Bell, Den Ouden, & Ziggers, 2006), *Journal of Management*, 43, 1607–1619 and labelled to be on the "bring of irrelevance". For theoretical and managerial reasons, networking the tourism industry calls for further scrutiny. Franchising offers a governance structure recognized for combining a valid business format and economies of scale provided by the franchisor with small entrepreneurs, who bring knowledge of local market and personal commitment to the joint action. Through a thorough interorganizational dynamics and franchising literature review, this study suggests that network governance mode holds promise of improving regional tourism industry performance.

1. Introduction

Tourism has become a networked industry in recent years. If a network can be defined as a set of actors, or nodes, and a set of relationships between them, then any touristic experience for the customer as well as any tourism activity for the service provider is networked. While a supply chain logic has traditionally been applied to study the tourism industry, patterns of interaction of more complex than a vertical value flow among firms also came to recognition (Baggio, Scott, & Cooper, 2010a). The upstream and downstream value creation logic revealed to oversimplify the diversity of interorganizational relationships and the network impact on the tourism industry. As a result, interaction structures, capabilities, and governance modes, collectively labelled as network distinctive phenomena have only recently come into research focus.

Within the management literature, networks earned strategic importance recognition long ago (Jarillo, 1988), and subsequent studies have clearly demonstrated their impact on gaining a competitive advantage (Donada, 2002). Collaboration can yield in terms of increased productivity, improved learning, better adaptation, or lower transaction costs, which bring relational rents to firms (Dyer & Singh, 1998). Also, networks generate distinctive effects that are not available in atomistic markets, or remain difficult to explain without focusing expressly on the network. Among those effects, unequal access to information and resources, social embeddedness of economic processes, contagion, and contingencies have attracted academic attention so far (Gulati, 1998). Each of those effects implies that some firms can achieve a better competitive position through networks against other firms, which opted to act individually on the market. A growing recognition of the importance of networks in firms' management research suggests that the study of the tourism industry can be expected to explain network distinctive effects, their antecedents, and influence on firms' performance as a prerequisite for a successful management of networks.

A closer scrutiny of the body of literature on networks in management reveals several foci of research: learning, the relationship characteristics, partnership success and alliance formation (Lin & Cheng, 2010). Furthermore, the literature explored the network governance modes (Jones, Hesterly, & Borgatti, 1997), their dynamics (Lowndes & Skelcher, 1998), and dominant types (Grandori & Soda, 1992). There is evidence that firms purposefully organize interfirm transactions in order to ensure collaboration efficiency and secure rents. Also, a significant thread of research has concentrated on network's structural variables in order to address performance heterogeneity (Baggio, Scott, & Cooper, 2010b). Generally put network structure, network governance, and network contingencies revealed to be significant explanatory variables of firm performance, development, and long-term success.

The objective of this paper is to further explore network theory (NT) applications to the tourism industry, by adopting a theoretical approach. A critical review of NT threads of research has been conducted from a structuralist perspective through governance issues, up to currently exploited capabilities approaches. While the structuralist perspective yielded so far insightful contributions to understanding how are structures conditioning action in networks, the network governance and capabilities appear in turn to be under-utilized in tourism management research. Consequently, the discussion part suggests a research agenda focused on the intentional design of networks. Business format franchise has been used to demonstrate both expected advantages and research gaps which undermine a more widespread use of networks in tourism research and management.

The paper is organized in five sections. First, industry networks are introduced, and the consequence of a network perspective for industry analysis is outlined. Second, collaboration advantages according to four theoretical perspectives are reviewed. Third, network governance mechanisms and dynamics are developed. Then, the franchising business model, seen here as a hierarchy dominant, centralized, and knowledge-exploitation-oriented network is described. Fifth, a discussion on why the franchising business format use in the tourism industry is limited has been developed. The lines of reasoning follow methodological, broker's role, and coordination cost issues.

2. Industry networks

The network form of organization has been spreading in several industries since the very beginning of the 1980s, as one of the managers has put it "there is a new beast in the jungle" (Miles & Snow, 1986). Further studies have focused on their characteristics (Gulati, Nohria, & Zaheer, 2000), dynamics (Bell, Den Ouden, & Ziggers, 2006), and the need to strategize around networks (Hakanson & Snehota, 2006). The general outcome of this thread of research is that acting in networks became a strategic imperative. Even if a firm does not deliberately shape its network, it is still embedded in a set of relationships which forms both a contingency, and a lever of action. Networks appeared to be a multifaceted phenomenon, understood as (1) structure or organization, (2) a resource coupled with distinctive capabilities, or a (3) coordination mode.

Second, networks are heterogeneous and yield different levels of performance at the network's and firm's level. While collaboration is generally seen as a source of advantages (Dyer & Sing, 1998), network characteristics such as cohesiveness or density may have a negative impact on businesses as well (Uzzi, 1997). Consequently, a thread of research focusing on the different levels of performance has been launched, and provided evidence that both the structures (Burt, 1992) and a distinctive capability to operate the network (Lorenzoni & Lipparini, 1999; Capaldo, 2007) shape firms' collaborative performance. Interestingly, structures alone do not appear to be in linear correlation with performance. In networks similar from a structural perspective, firms often display different levels of performance. This particularity has justified an increasing perception of networks as resources, which generate value when coupled with capabilities. While competitive advantage may stem from resources, firms still need to know how to use them at their advantage.

Third, researchers approached networks from a transaction cost economics (TCE) perspective in order to better understand the network mode of coordination. In fact networks offer quite distinctive contingencies to managers, as different partners are not under direct hierarchical subordination, making traditional organization theory and its bureaucratic control tools of limited usefulness. Similarly, networks differ from arms-length market transactions. Networked actors repeatedly interact and commit to their interaction beyond the requirements of one single market transaction. Furthermore, significant importance has been attributed to trust and social norms in coordinating action of collaborating firms (Ouchi, 1980). Thus, networks are seen as a mode of coordination of different modes from market or hierarchies, though not exclusively based on social mechanism, instead making use of all three available modes (Poppo & Zenger, 2002).

In sum, the role of networks in management has been recognized from different stances. Researchers attribute positive effects on efficiency, learning, and adaptation to networks. However, there is also evidence that the network requires careful coordination and capabilities in order to perform.

3. Collaborative advantages

Firms collaborate with others in order to achieve results which remain beyond their individual reach or would require a significant level of resource commitment coupled with high risk (Koza & Lewin, 1999). Researchers typically adopt several theoretical stances: the industry organization (IO) theory, the resource-based view (RBV) of the firm, the NT, and the TCE.

The IO stance in strategic management contends that firms' performance is shaped by the industry structure (Porter, 1980) and the position a firm is able to work out within it. Major factors in this structure are captured as bargaining power, resulting from size and relative concentration in the buyer–supplier relationship. The stronger a firm is, the bigger share of available value it will get. While organic growth or mergers and acquisitions require time and substantial resources, alliances can leverage firm's potential on the market. Horizontal alliances provide first-mover advantages, increase the individual firm's bargaining power by combining it with the power of its partners, induce other players to follow, and act as a countering device (Garcia-Point & Nohria, 2002). In other words, networks come to challenge the atomistic assumptions underlying industry analysis. However useful it can be, industry structure uses a set approach, where performance results from power, and power results from relative concentration upstream or downstream of the supply chain. Therefore, firms often opt for collaboration, which creates clusters of coordinated action and privileged terms of exchange. Networks appear here as a means of countering industry structure impact by installing coordination. It is noteworthy to underline that this theory uses an agglomeration approach, grounded in industry economics dating back to the XIV century, and does not explore further structural, functional, or resource antecedents to collaborative advantage.

Another theoretical approach uses the resource interdependence of firms in order to justify alliance and network formation. The RBV claims that no firm is self-sufficient in terms of resources, or capabilities it needs to deliver its customers the value they expect. Moreover, resource mobility and availability are typically not perfect. Therefore, it often appears too costly, too risky, or simply impossible to either buy or develop firm's own resource base (Katila, Rosenberger, & Eisenhardt, 2008). Real market conditions leave managers out of the "buy or make" dilemma, as both options become unrealistic. Under those circumstances firms can still consider alliances, which beyond providing resources yield also a relative advantage of accessing resources while other market players remain out of access (Gulati, 1998).

Nevertheless, firms acting in networks achieve different results. Thus, networks cannot be considered as panacea, or black boxes, which always work. Firm's capabilities have been exploited by researchers in order to elucidate the network heterogeneity issue (Jarrat, 2004). Another argument links the capabilities to structures (Blyler & Coff, 2003). A relational capability can be viewed at dyadic level, addressing the ability to efficiently working with a specific partner (Rodriguez-Diaz & Espino-Rodriguez, 2006b). At the network level, it reaches for more elaborate competencies, as the whole network: (1) has to be created, (2) then its resources mobilized and its operation stabilized (Lorenzoni & Lipparini, 1999), (3) conflict resolution mechanisms implemented, and (4) rent appropriation regime accepted by collaborating parties (Dhanaraj & Parkhe, 2006). Such sets of capabilities are referred to as orchestration, but still remain at an early stage of theoretical explanation. Nevertheless, it is clear in the literature that a purposefully shaped network needs a leader, whose most visible role is to shape a governance structure for collaboration.

The NT exploits structural variables in order to elucidate how relationships influence firm's behaviours and performance. The adoption of structural contingency approach has allowed to model communication processes in sociology (Burt, 1992), disease diffusion in populations in epidemiology, to leverage collective resources in order to achieve competitive advantage in industrial economics (Lorenzoni & Baden-Fuller, 1995), or to explain business strategies (Hakansson & Snehota, 2006). The diffusion concept has been further exploited in knowledge flow studies (Huggins & Johnston, 2010) or mimetic processes (Galaskiewicz & Wassermann, 1996), which leads to a uniformity of behaviours, routines, and ultimately performance.

Network embedding of firm's activities is not a given or independent contingency, but results from deliberate decisions. One of the most popular arguments is that those ties that are bridging structural holes in networks provide the firm with a privileged situation (Burt, 1992). A structural hole is a discontinuity in the network structure, a separation between non-redundant contacts. When a firm bridges structural holes, it can use richer sets of information, resources, and capabilities or actions, which benefit both for the connected networks and the bridging firm itself. In turn, learning about new opportunities is facilitated by weak ties, characterized by low frequency of contact and low emotional commitment. Also, central positions in networks allow for coordination of knowledge creation and exploitation (Dyer & Hatch, 2004).

Interestingly, some authors (Reagans & Zuckerman, 2001) suggest that convergence in networks does not necessarily imply the choice of the best performing routine. A lock-in effect of low-performing routines can also appear. In summary, this thread of research tends to consider networks as a contingencies and levers for information diffusion.

The TCE, in turn, emphasizes that relational contracting provides better efficiency of coordination, as compared to hierarchies or markets (Jones et al., 1997). Rich information exchange becomes possible when parties trust each other, and are committed in the long term to operate jointly. Negotiating future terms of collaboration allows for relationship-specific investments, which typically enhance synergies between firms. Also, mutual learning allows to increase efficiencies of networked actions (Dyer & Singh, 1998). Empirical research provides evidence that networks boost performance (McEvily & Zaheer, 1999), the likelihood of firm's survival (Baum, Calabrese, & Silverman, 2000), and improve sales (Podolny, Stuart, & Hannan, 1996).

Networks can be source of advantages to firms due to increased market power, access to resources, learning, and efficient coordination. A substantial body of literature in the NT provides evidence on structural relationships with performance. However, there is evidence that structures or resources alone do not act as stand-alone variables. Firms need to display relational and network capabilities, referring to the know-how of cooperation.

4. Network governance

The network governance combines three modes of governing transactions: market, hierarchy, and clan (Ouchi, 1980), extensively drawing from the TCE. Theoretical reference to TCE implies a focus on opportunism and deterrence mechanism, which add to the cost of using a specific coordination mechanism.

Market governance relies on the price mechanism to coordinate actors' actions and allocate resources. However, the behavioural contingencies of contracting such as bounded rationality or opportunism induce the need to use formal contracts in order to specify mutual expectations, the rules of collaboration, and conflict resolution options. The market or price mechanism is therefore generating transaction costs, and calls for a third-party intervention for conflict resolution. The transaction costs are reducing the price mechanism's efficiency, and are used in the neo-institutional economics to justify the need for the existence of firms. The firm is needed because under some circumstances including institutional environment, opportunism, size, the frequency of transactions, and so on, the cost of coordinating transactions by the market mechanism becomes prohibitively high. An oversimplified understanding of transaction costs economics may induce a false belief that depending on transaction cost level firms would appear or disappear.

Hierarchy refers to bureaucratic mechanisms of coordinating actions and allocating resources. It relies on standard operating procedures, control systems, and a legal authority that both controls the actions of subordinates and offers a conflict-resolution mechanism. While bureaucratic governance is attributed to firms, it should be underlined that also interfirm relations are often framed using mechanisms typical to hierarchy, notably within franchising networks (Czakon, 2009a). Similarly to market coordination, under some conditions, the hierarchical coordination becomes too costly. Moreover, firms do not find bureaucratic coordination to foster entrepreneurship, autonomy, or innovation (Fulop & Forward, 1997).

Clans or relational governance relies, in turn, on trust and social norms of accepted behaviour. Trust can most succinctly be stressed as the belief that partners will be previsible, committed, credible, good-willing, reciprocal, and deterred from opportunistic behaviours (Kohtamaki, Vesalainen, Varamaki, & Vuorinen, 2005). Trust drives open and rich information transfer, allowing partners to make better decisions and better coordinate their actions that actors outside the networks (Jones et al., 1997). Social norms, in turn, provide a self-enforcing mechanism, as the partners would face social sanctions if their actions would infringe accepted boundaries. To a large extent, researchers assume social norms to be the substitutes to contractual agreements. However, empirical evidence suggests rather that social norms act as a complementary mechanism to the contractual one (Poppo & Zenger, 2002).

A distinctive feature of network governance is that it combines all three mechanisms instead of opting for one ideal-type mode of framing transactions: "coordination characterized by informal social systems rather than by bureaucratic structures within firms and formal contractual relationships between them" (Jones et al., 1997). While the use of social mechanisms appears to be a distinctive feature for network governance, it does not necessarily imply that collaborating firms abandon contracts or hierarchies. Therefore, a need for purposeful balance setting between the mechanisms and further adaptation emerges (Jap & Ganesan, 2000). Networks will differ depending on whether hierarchy, social, or market mechanism are dominant, and the network leader needs to take account for both network and environment contingencies (Joshi & Campbell, 2003).

Depending on the relationship life cycle, authors have found different sequences of dominant governance within network settings. Basing on the assumption that networks emerge from socially embedded relationships, some authors suggest that the social mechanism is followed by hierarchy (Larson, 1992). Others provided evidence that hierarchy is then followed by a market mechanism, only to turn back to social coordination (Lowndes & Skelcher, 1998). Yet, networks can be intentionally designed, then hierarchy would be the starting point (Jap & Ganesan, 2000). While the need to purposefully shape governance mechanisms balance has been recognized, there are few empirical studies that tackle this issue.

Following the heterogeneity argument in strategic management, different governance choices yield different performance levels. The literature suggests the need to purposefully shape network governance structures. Therefore, collaboration efficiency is related to how network governance evolves, becoming both a composite and dynamic concept. Within this field of scrutiny, a relatively limited number of studies adopted the governance approach. While networks as structures and resources have so far been largely exploited, their organization mode remains far from being conclusive.

5. Business format franchising

Organization theorists and the strategy literature have been long focusing on the argument that organizations should differ in order to achieve success on a competitive market, making replication a neglected topic of academic attention (Winter & Szulanski, 2001).

Nevertheless, replication offers significant advantages for firms. Among them knowledge transfer on technological, organizational, behavioural, and other relevant issues of running the business replication are frequently listed. Interestingly, mutual learning in a network environment reveals to be beneficial both to the central actor, who receives detailed information on relevant business contingencies, and the peripheral actors, who benefit from a standardized knowledge transfer and learning support. Therefore, replication appears as a valuable tool for the replicator, and for those who replicate. The literature suggests also that successful replication requires templates, and that systems and operating procedures provide a considerable advantage, while creating strong inter-dependencies between actors. Consequently, in a networked industry such as tourism, strategies which foster the diffusion of knowledge bring network communities of practice (Brown & Duguid, 2001). Prior research suggests that knowledge can easily move across organizational boundaries and network connections are likely to bring a convergence in the routines operated by networked organizations.

Franchising is a multifaceted phenomenon and encompasses a wide variety of forms, scopes, and network sizes. Generally, under franchising contracts, the franchisee is granted a license to sell the franchisor's products or services, and also benefits from a standard business system, proven operating methods, support, and advice, while remaining legally distinct firms (Fulop & Forward, 1997). These authors distinguish three phases of franchising development, the business format franchising being the latest, most developed, and widespread. Firms are opting for franchising for several reasons: organizational, socioeconomic, and reputation.

Organizational reasons refer to the benefits of operating in a networked environment. It is important to distinguish two levels of analysis: the network and the individual actor. At the network level of analysis, franchising is a rapid way of expansion and gaining market size, in other words, a way of scaling up in order to achieve scale economies and a visible market position. At individual level, different advantages accrue to the franchisor and the franchisees.

For the central agent, franchising is a low-capital intensive, rapid way of expanding on the market, which contributes to gaining and sustaining competitive advantage (Czakon, 2009b). On the other hand, the franchisees are able to significantly reduce risk of setting up a business, and benefit from a strong marketing, technological, and operating support after the business formation.

Socioeconomic factors for franchising development include an increased role of entrepreneurship and the strive for autonomy. The latter problem has traditionally been studied from agency theory stances. Prior research provides evidence that under hierarchical governance, innovation, flexibility and proactive behaviour are much more difficult to generate than in separate firms (Doherty & Quinn, 1999). Thus, while offering a standardized product, strong quality control to customer's business franchising is linking entrepreneurs to a hierarchical firm. Both are able to benefit from the advantages difficult to obtain under their specific contingencies – the entrepreneur receives hierarchical control systems helping to efficiently manage his activities, while the franchisor obtains entrepreneurial spirit within his hierarchy.

The third-party influence arises from reputation, as small firms operating under a franchisor logo are considered to be less risky than comparable firms working under a proprietary logo. Seen from a network governance perspective, the franchising structure is dominated by hierarchical control. Franchisees receive plans of action similar to budgets, or at least are controlled for the results achieved. Their turnover is being closely supervised, as the franchising fee typically represents a proportion of income. Also, their operating procedures are closely audited through mystery shopper and other types of techniques. Franchisee's employees receive standard training provided by the franchisor. Finally, from a power perspective, there is a strong asymmetry between the central actor who has the authority to invite an entrepreneur into the network but also to expel him. Nevertheless, market mechanism and some social mechanism also can be observed within franchising networks, although for a lesser extent.

In this study, we contend that a hierarchy-dominated network governance calls for a closer scrutiny in tourism industry settings. Several reasons justify this claim. Firstly, franchising means intentional network creation in order to replicate a bundle of routines on the market. Designed processes tend to foster knowledge diffusion and routine adoption, likely to create a network advantage for collaborating businesses. Secondly, hierarchical relationships emphasize the stability of operations, bringing efficiency, and control ease. Therefore, it becomes simple to control for the quality or quantity of output, as well as for the processes deployed in order to achieve expected results. Thirdly, franchising respects the formal independence of firms, mostly small or medium sized. This corresponds to the typical structure of the tourism industry, composed to a large extent of small and medium enterprises (SMEs) cooperating with a few larger operators. Fourthly, franchising promotes market identification by a single branding approach. Reputation and identity are to a large extent in focus within the tourism industry, and are widely used as a basis for differentiation and further to competitive advantage. In summary, franchising may be perceived as an advantageous way of governing network relationships.

6. Discussion

In the tourism industry, many actors operate on different services: transport, accommodation, restaurants, cultural events, sport activities, rental, insurance, etc. Their activities are closely linked and remain to various extents interdependent. For instance, while some tour operators have risen to become brokers of the whole industry, tourist on site are free to choose, and often opt for services provided beyond the core tour operator network. In other words, the specialization, interdependency, and final product complexity allows for scrutinizing the tourism industry from a network perspective. More than that, the strategic management literature findings on networks implicitly encourage networks formation.

Networks in tourism can be analysed at two geographical levels: local and regional. At the local level in tourist locations, clustering effects of agglomerating many firms connected with tourist services are typical. At the regional level the brokers, or tour operators, provide linkages between air transport, tourist, hotels, restaurants, and other services. Brokers benefit from structural holes in the network, as tourists are disconnected from service providers, and inversely once this connection is being made the need for an operator decreases.

Business format franchising can reasonably be expected to benefit the tourism industry by providing reputation, survival, and scale effects. The consumers can use the franchising logo as a brand that ensures them about the quality of service. Entering into the franchising network also provides bigger survival chances for the entrepreneur. Also the actors can benefit from scale effects while buying supplies, furniture, materials, and other products necessary for their operations.

Should franchising be so beneficial for the tourism industry the problem arises why it is not widespread? Following the qualitative comparative analysis method (Kogut & Ragin, 2006), this question addresses those features of a theoretically possible set that are not observable empirically. In doing so, researchers unveil contingencies that make only a limited set of features possible from among their theoretical diversity. Therefore, a first suggestion arises for future research agenda, regarding the research method to be used. Industry specific factors, linked to tourism exclusively to tourism should be explored to unveil the reasons of current governance choices, at the expense of theoretically more viable ones.

Also, endogenous factors such as capabilities need to be scrutinized. As reviewed before, the network leader needs distinct capabilities in order to frame a network. Franchising requires an even much more specific leader that provides proven systems and operating procedures, support, and is credible on the market. This leads to the second future research question regarding the networking capabilities required in tourism. Prior research on hotels (Rodriguez-Diaz & Espino-Rodriguez, 2006a) provides evidence that networking capability is important for hotel's performance. Yet, the way to go from recognition to a more fine-tuned understanding of the network capability in tourism understanding calls for further scrutiny.

Franchising implies power asymmetries between the central agent and those connected to it by franchising contracts. Asymmetry issues may be more acute in the tourism industry, because it is localized and seasonal. Therefore, resources of entrepreneurs are very difficult if possible at all to move, while those resources need to be mobilized and yield for the time after the season. Under those circumstances, a third question arises on what power asymmetry is acceptable for entrepreneurs.

In sum, some theoretical tensions arise when confronting the current industry practice with theoretical insight. Governance, capability, and industry-specific factors can be expected to contribute to a better understanding of tourism industry network governance, and to yield reasonable likelihood of improvement.

7. Conclusion and implications

Networked industries can display different levels of performance depending on endogenous and exogenous factors. Endogenous factors refer to the network structure, governance, and value proposition orchestrated typically by a network leader. Most widespread networks use standard ways of operating under business format franchising. Exogenous factors are connected with resource mobility, business contingencies, and third-party expectations. By analogy to retail and service industries, a strong potential resides in franchising for tourism, especially for locations that otherwise need for credibility, scale effects, and organization. This suggests that developing tourist regions would be more interested than established ones.

Beyond resource and market power considerations, collaborative advantages of networks are connected with the way firms interact with each other. Network governance calls for a purposefully shaped and balanced use of the social, hierarchical, and market mechanism. More than just governing transactions, network governance leads to the creation of business ecosystems. The efficiency of transactions, a rapid replication of high-performing routines, mutual learning, co-specialization can thus thrive and foster global competitive advantages. Business format franchising can contribute to rapidly install such an ecosystem, provide guidance, and support for its members and develop the tourism industry.

While franchising offers considerable advantages, it also displays some drawbacks and reticence among tourism entrepreneurs. Among them, power asymmetries and resulting from it rent appropriation regimes are of particular concern. Research on networking the tourism industry can be expected to scrutinize boundary conditions, capabilities, and processes for industry-specific networks to thrive. In other service industries, the search for a successful mix in business format franchising has taken decades. Nevertheless, a significant portion of services industry growth and global expansion is attributed to franchising. Seen from this perspective, the creation of global tourism networks operating under one brand, common standards, and within cohesive business ecosystems require further studies and implementation efforts.

References

Baggio, R., Scott, N., & Cooper, C. (2010a). Network science: A review focused on tourism. *Annals of Tourism Research, 37*, 802–827.

Baggio, R., Scott, N., & Cooper, C. (2010b). Improving tourism destination governance: A complexity science approach. *Tourism Review*, *65*, 51–60.

Baum, J., Calabrese, T., & Silverman, B. (2000). Don't go it alone: Alliance network composition and startups' performance in Canadian biotechnology. *Strategic Management Journal*, *21*, 267–294.

Bell, J., Den Ouden, B., & Ziggers, G. (2006). Dynamics of cooperation: At the brink of irrelevance. *Journal of Management*, *43*, 1607–1619.

Blyler, M., & Coff, R. (2003). Dynamic capabilities, social capital and rent appropriation: Ties that split pies. *Strategic Management Journal*, *24*, 677–686.

Brown, J., & Duguid, P. (2001). Knowledge and organization: A social practice perspective. *Organization Science*, *12*, 198–213.

Burt, R. (1992). *Structural holes – the social structure of competition*. Cambridge, MA: Harvard University Press.

Capaldo, A. (2007). Network structure and innovation: The leveraging of a dual network as a distinctive relational capability. *Strategic Management Journal*, *28*, 585–608.

Czakon, W. (2009a). Network governance dynamics impact on intellectual property management: The case of a franchise system. *International Journal of Intellectual Property Management*, *3*, 23–38.

Czakon, W. (2009b). Power asymmetries, flexibility and the propensity to coopete: An empirical investigation of SMEs' relationships with franchisors. *International Journal of Entrepreneurship and Small Business*, *8*, 44–60.

Dhanaraj, C., & Parkhe, A. (2006). Orchestrating innovation networks. *Academy of Management Review*, *31*, 659–669.

Doherty, A., & Quinn, B. (1999). International retail franchising: An agency theory perspective. *International Journal of Retail & Distribution Management*, *27*, 224–236.

Donada, C. (2002). Generating cooperative gain in a vertical partnership: A supplier's perspective. *Canadian Journal of Administrative Sciences*, *19*, 173–183.

Dyer, J., & Hatch, N. (2004). Using supplier networks to learn faster. *MIT Sloan Management Review*, *45*, 57–63.

Dyer, J., & Singh, H. (1998). The relational view: Cooperative strategy and sources of interorganizational competitive advantage. *The Academy of Management Review*, *24*, 660–679.

Fulop, C., & Forward, J. (1997). Insights into franchising: A review of empirical and theoretical perspectives. *The Services Industries Journal*, *17*, 603–625.

Galaskiewicz, J., Wasserman, S. (1989). Mimetic processes within an interorganizational field. *Administrative Science Quarterly*, *34*, 454–479.

Garcia-Point, C., & Nohria, N. (2002). Local versus global mimetism: The dynamics of alliance formation in the automobile industry. *Strategic Management Journal*, *23*, 307–321.

Grandori, A., & Soda, G. (1992). Inter-firm networks: Antecedents, mechanisms and forms. *Organization Studies*, *16*, 183–214.

Gulati, R. (1998). Alliances and networks. *Strategic Management Journal*, *19*, 293–317.

Gulati, R., Nohria, N., & Zaheer, A. (2000). Strategic networks. *Strategic Management Journal*, *21*, 203–215.

Hakanson, H., & Snehota, I. (2006). No business is an island: The network concept of business strategy. *Scandinavian Journal of Management*, *5*, 187–200.

Huggins R., and Johnston A. (2010): Knowledge flow and inter-firm networks: the influence of network resources, spatial proximity and firm size. *Entrepreneurship & Regional Development*, Vol. 22, 457–484.

Jap, S., & Ganesan, S. (2000). Control mechanisms and the relationship life cycle: Implications for safeguarding specific investments and developing commitment. *Journal of Marketing Research*, *37*, 227–245.

Jarillo, J.C. (1988). On strategic networks. *Strategic Management Journal*, *9*, 31–41.

Jarrat, D. (2004). Conceptualizing a relationship management capability. *Marketing Theory*, *4*, 287–309.

Jones, C., Hesterly, W., & Borgatti, S. (1997). A general theory of network governance: Exchange conditions and social mechanisms. *Academy of Management Review*, *22*, 911–945.

Joshi, A., & Campbell, J. (2003). Effect of environmental dynamism on relational governance in manufacturer-supplier relationships: A contingent framework and an empirical test. *Academy of Marketing Science Journal*, *31*, 176–188.

Katila, R., Rosenberger, J.D., & Eisenhardt, K. (2008). Swimming with the sharks: Technology ventures, defense mechanisms and corporate relationships. *Administrative Science Quarterly, 53*, 295–332.

Kogut, B., & Ragin, C. (2006). Exploring complexity when diversity is limited: Institutional complementarity in theories of rule of law and national systems revisited. *European Management Review, 3*, 44–59.

Kohtamaki, M., Vesalainen, J., Varamaki, E., & Vuorinen, T. (2005). The governance of partnerships and a strategic network: Supplier actors' experiences in the governance by the customers. *Management Decision, 44*, 1031–1051.

Koza, M.P., & Lewin, A.Y. (1999). The coevolution of network alliances: A longitudinal analysis of an international professional service network. *Organization Science, 10*, 638–653.

Larson, A. (1992). Network dyads in entrepreneurial settings: A study of the governance of exchange relationships. *Administrative Science Quarterly, 37*, 76–105.

Lin, T.Y., & Cheng, Y.Y. (2010). Exploring the knowledge network of strategic alliance research: A co-citation analysis. *International Journal of Electronic Business Management, 8*, 152–160.

Lorenzoni G., Baden-Fuller C. (1995). Creating a strategic center to manager a web of partners. *California Management Review, 37*, 146–163.

Lorenzoni, G., & Lipparini, A. (1999). The leveraging of interfirm relationships as a distinctive organizational capability: A longitudinal study. *Strategic Management Journal, 20*, 317–338.

Lowndes, V., & Skelcher, C. (1998). The dynamics of multi-organizational partnerships: An analysis of changing modes of governance. *Public Administration, 76*, 313–333.

McEvily, B., & Zaheer, A. (1999). Bridging ties: A source of firm heterogeneity in competitive abilities. *Strategic Management Journal, 20*, 1133–1153.

Miles, R., & Snow, C. (1986). Network organizations: New concepts for new forms. *McKinsey Quarterly, 3*, 53–66.

Ouchi, W. (1980). Markets, bureaucracies and clans. *Administrative Science Quarterly, 25*, 129–141.

Podolny, J., Stuart, T., & Hannan, M. (1996). Networks, knowledge and niches: Competition in the worldwide semiconductor industry 1984-1991. *The American Journal of Sociology, 102*, 659–689.

Poppo, L., & Zenger, T. (2002). Do formal contracts and relational governance function as substitutes or complements? *Strategic Management Journal, 23*, 707–725.

Porter, M.E. (1980). *Strategy. Techniques for analyzing industries and competitors.* New York: The Free Press.

Porter, M.E. (1990). *The competitive advantage of nations.* Free Press, New York.

Reagans, R., & Zuckerman, E. (2001). Networks, diversity and productivity: The social capital of corporate R&D teams. *Organization Science, 12*, 502–517.

Rodriguez-Diaz, M., & Espino-Rodriguez, T. (2006a). Developing relational capabilities in hotels. *International Journal of Contemporary Hospitality Management, 18*, 25–40.

Rodriguez-Diaz, M., & Espino-Rodriguez, T. (2006b). Redesigning the supply chain: Reengineering, outsourcing and relational capabilities. *Business Process Management Journal, 12*, 483–502.

Uzzi, B. (1997). Social structure and competition in interfirm networks: The paradox of embeddedness. *Administrative Science Quarterly, 42*, 35–67.

Winter, S., & Szulanski, G. (2001). Replication as strategy. *Organization Science, 12*, 730–743.

Index

Page numbers in **bold** type refer to figures
Page numbers in *italic* type refer to tables
Page numbers followed by 'n' refer to notes